SPINNER MAGIC!

The Ultimate Moving-Water Lure
Trout · Steelhead · Salmon

Jim Bedford

Frank Amato
PUBLICATIONS, INC.

About the Author

Jim Bedford is a retired environmental scientist who lives in southern Michigan with his wife of 45 years, Kathel. He has two grown children and fishes often with his daughter, Terri. He is an extremely avid river angler and spends more than 1,000 hours a year wading streams, fishing for steelhead, trout, and salmon. While he concentrates his fishing in Michigan he regularly travels to the rivers of other states and provinces. An award-winning author and photographer, Jim Bedford has been writing for over 35 years and has written for *Field & Stream*, *Outdoor Life*, *Salmon Trout Steelheader*, and *Trout*, as well as numerous regional and Michigan publications. *Spinner Magic!* is his fourth book.

All inquiries should be addressed to:
Frank Amato Publications, Inc. • P.O. Box 82112 • Portland, Oregon 97282
(503) 653-8108
www.AmatoBooks.com

Book & Cover Design by Mariah Hinds
Spinner Photographs by Mariah Hinds (pages: 1-4, 6, 9, 16, 20, 26, 32, 35, 42, 47, 53, 60, 65, 69)
Photography by Author Unless Otherwise Noted
Illustrations by Dürten Kampmann
ISBN 10: 1-57188-460-2
ISBN-13: 978-1-57188-460-2
UPC: 0-81127-00299-3
Printed in China

10 9 8 7 6 5 4 3 2 1

SPINNER
MAGIC!

Contents

Chapter 1
Why Fish Spinners? 6

Chapter 2
Spinner-Fishing Tackle & Techniques 9

Rods 10
Reels 10
Line 11
Loading Your Vest or Tackle Box 12
Spinner-fishing Techniques 14
Rigging 15

Chapter 3
Matching the Conditions 16

Metal Reflectivity 19

Chapter 4
Reading & Covering Water 20

Decoding the River 21
Moving Right Along 23

Chapter 5
Aggressive & Safe Wading 26

Waders.. 26
Wading & Wading Helpers............ 28
Wader Repair & Care.................... 30

Chapter 6
Fishing Spinners from a Floating Craft 32

Stealth 33
The Bottom Up............................. 33
Complementary Techniques 34
Float to Wade............................... 34

Chapter 7
Steelhead Biology & Habits;
Best Spinners & Techniques 35

The Fish 36
Early Stream Life 36
Ocean & Big Lake......................... 36
Different Mixes 37
Migration Rate 38
Do They Feed? 38

Steelhead or Lake-Run Rainbow 39
Best Spinner & Tactics 41

Chapter 8
Salmon Biology & Habits;
Best Spinners & Techniques 42

Chinook Salmon 43
Coho Salmon................................ 44
Pink Salmon 44
Sockeye Salmon............................ 45
Chum Salmon 46

Chapter 9
Trout Biology & Habits;
Best Spinners & Techniques 47

Rainbow Trout............................... 48
Cutthroat Trout 48
Brown Trout 49
Brook Trout 50
Dolly Varden Trout........................ 51
Resident Trout Tactics 51

Chapter 10
Making Your Own Spinners 53

Blades 54
Shafts... 55
Spinner Bodies 56
Hooks 56
Putting Them Together 57
Preventing Spinner Loss................. 59

Chapter 11
Landing & Releasing 60

Hooking, Fighting, & Landing 61
Releasing 62

Chapter 12
Cast & Retrieve Alternatives 65

Spoons 65
Plugs.. 66

Chapter 13
Putting it All Together 69

CHAPTER 1

Why Fish Spinners?

The spinner felt just right as it swept across the holding water. The current kept the blade turning at a slow speed and the current felt just right for what I had learned steelhead like to hold in over many years of fishing for them. Occasionally I could feel the blade tick the gravel but most of the time the spinner was up off the bottom. Suddenly there was no water resistance and I raised my rod. Feeling solid resistance I sharply finished the hook-set and felt the wonderful throb of a head-shaking steelhead. The frisky anadromous rainbow split its time between leaping out of the river and making line sizzling runs before being corralled in my net. Without touching the fish or lifting the net bag from the water I twisted the spinner free, lowered the net rim and let the steelie swim free.

If it seemed like you read 'feel' or 'felt' in almost every sentence above you probably did. The reason is that spinner-fishing is all about feel. At a time when it seems like most methods for catching steelhead, trout, and salmon involve watching a float or strike indicator, or your rod tip, or the dry fly itself, spinner-fishing is about utilizing your sense of touch to the max. The revolving spinner blade creates a resistance in the water so you can feel your spinner working; you put this resistance to use to know that the blade is turning. When sweeping across the river the resistance will help you feel how strong the current is and changes in it due to obstructions such as big boulders. Soon you learn the strength of current that salmon and steelhead prefer. You will also be able to detect fish-holding cover as the blade ticks the top of a rock or log. The most fun is feeling the strike of a fish. Strikes range from trout or salmon trying to remove the rod from your hand to very subtle takes as described above.

The weighted spinner is a very versatile lure. It can be successfully fished cast straight upstream or across or down. One reason is that it has action (spins) at a very slow retrieve, especially those spinners made with broad, French type blades and the other is that it sinks rapidly. High-action plugs also have action at a slow retrieve but it's hard to get them down unless they are run directly against the current. You can control the depth your spinner is running by the speed of the retrieve and the position of your rod tip. This allows you to work the spinner into all kinds of fish-holding nooks and crannies in a stream or river.

Casting accuracy is important when river fishing, especially when you are chasing resident trout in streams with lots of cover. Compact weighted spinners are one of the easiest lures to toss to the "spot". There is no "helicoptering" of drift lure or bait and the sinker, like there is when drift fishing. If you add a float, the casting gets even more difficult. Less dense lures like plugs, especially the balsa minnow types, will often "sail" off course. The fly-angler has to keep track of the line, leader, and fly to put his or her offering on target. Flipping spinners into tight places is lots of fun and helps show your lure to more fish than other techniques.

Spinner-tossing is a very hands-on active way to fish for trout and salmon. You are always in the process of casting and retrieving or guiding and feeling your spinner working through the holding water. Bottom-bouncing or drifting without a float is similar except that the current is presenting the offering and you rarely

cover as much water. You cover lots of water when side drifting in a boat but the oarsman or motor operator is doing all the fishing and the angler is just manning the rod. The same is true when pulling plugs from a boat. Because you are not completely at the mercy of the current when you are casting and retrieving spinners you can fish lots of snaggy holding water and other nooks and crannies that the drift angler can't.

Another plus for fishing spinners is that they tend to catch larger fish, especially anadromous fish. A case can be made for the possibility that larger steelhead and salmon are more territorial. They were that way as they grew into smolts in the river, enabling them to be a bit larger before they headed for the ocean or Great Lakes. They used their larger size for a better start in the big water. Since spinners don't resemble any food item and usually evoke a take by invading the territory of anadromous fish, the "boss salmonid" is likely to try and take it out. Resident trout are also territorial. While the spinner still doesn't represent a specific food to them it does represent something alive and a substantial meal so may draw the attention of trout at the top of the pecking order.

An additional positive about invading an anadromous fish's territory with a gaudy spinner is that it evokes a better fight, on average, from the steelhead or salmon. In response to the hard hook-set, the fish seems to say, "Okay, if you want to play rough, we'll play rough." The dangling metal from their jaws seems to be quite

You never know what you'll encounter when you travel a river tossing spinners, "moose crossing".

irritating, causing steelhead and other leapers to jump more, and all species to pull really hard. I am also guessing that the stronger force applied by the comparably stiffer rod and stronger line panics them somewhat.

A real attraction of spinner-fishing is its simplicity. You don't need to be concerned with leaders, swivels, sinkers, fresh or properly cured bait, yarn, or floats. You just tie on a spinner and start casting. Your only challenge is to pick a size and blade finish that arouses the curiosity of a stream trout and entices it to eat it or gets the anadromous fish's attention and aggravates it into striking. You don't want your spinner being ignored because the fish don't notice it or are spooked because it's too bright for the conditions. We will spend a whole chapter helping you pick the right spinner.

If these are not reasons enough, the final and most important reason is that they really catch salmon, trout, and steelhead. Brown trout, especially large specimens, are arguably the smartest and wariest of the trout and salmon family. Early in my trout fishing career I had a large brown follow my spinner out from an undercut bank several times without striking. Giving it one more try I let the spinner sink to the bottom before beginning the retrieve and the trout was on it in a flash. Unfortunately I was unable to keep my orange-bellied adversary from making it into a log-jam just upstream and

it went around a log and broke me off. Disappointed, I climbed the bank to get around the jam and flipped my spinner into the pool above the jam. Immediately a large brown grabbed it and I was able to land this one. As I went to unhook the 20-incher I discovered it had two spinners in its mouth. A once-in-a-lifetime freak event, right?

Well, a few years later in a very tight brushy stream a big brown grabbed my spinner and I set the hook hard. The rod tip went into the tag alder over my head and the line broke at the rod tip. Knowing that there would be a long trail of line in the water, I tied on another spinner and cast it upstream hoping to catch the trailing line. Instead the spinner was attacked by a trout, and after a tense battle a 22-inch trophy was corralled in my net with two identical brass spinners in its mouth. I would expect these scenarios to be possible with live bait but not with identical artificial lures. Obviously, the spinner was really irresistible in these instances.

I am obviously biased but I think the weighted spinner is the ultimate moving-water lure. It will also catch fish in lakes and ponds, but it really shines when there is current. One thing you can count on, if your spinner spins it will catch members of the trout and salmon family.

Large brown that grabbed a spinner.

CHAPTER 2

Spinner-Fishing Tackle & Techniques

Both spinning and casting gear can be used to fish rivers with weighted spinners. Steelhead and salmon fishermen tend to use casting gear when fishing with lures, especially in the Pacific Northwest. Spinning gear is more popular in the Great Lakes for anadromous fish and most trout anglers anywhere will use spinning tackle to toss lures. We will discuss both, but a case will be made for using spinning gear when fishing weighted spinners.

Rod with a long fore grip and short butt grip alongside a pretty brookie.

Rods

A spinner-tossing rod has to be light and limber enough to cast the lures well and be stiff enough to set a rather heavy-wire hook into a fairly tough jaw, especially salmon on their run up the river. To get both qualities choose a light to medium rod with a fast to extra-fast taper to a fairly heavy butt section. The rods I use for salmon and steelhead are only seven to eight feet long but that is a little deceiving. They are spinning rods and I build them with a very short butt section, only about three inches. Thus their effective length compares to factory-built rods, with their long butt sections, which are seven and a half to nine feet in length. Factory-made casting rods tend to have even longer butt sections.

Trout rods need to be a bit more limber to cast light lures and don't need quite the hook-setting power. My most-used spinning rods for stream-resident trout are six and a half feet in length with a light action and just a fast taper. They are also built with a short butt section. Many anglers like very short, five feet or even less, ultra-light rods for trout fishing. Rods a foot or so longer will serve you better when tossing spinners for trout. You need the extra length to make good underhand, pendulum casts that we will be talking about soon.

Graphite is the preferred material but you don't need or want rods with the super-light, super-high-modulus graphite. While sensitivity is very important when feeling what your spinner is doing or detecting subtle takes, regular (96%) or second-generation (IM-6) graphite will suffice. Higher-modulus graphite material is generally too fragile for spinner-fishing. There will be lots of very hard strikes and vigorous hook-sets that will strain the rod. And there will be times when the spinner slams into the rod, usually when the trout or salmon comes unhooked at close range, firing the chunk of metal right at the rod. Even if the rod doesn't break on impact it will be weakened at that spot and may break on a hook-set several trips later.

Cork grips and graphite reel seats over graphite arbors will help you feel your lure working. My rods are strange looking in that they have cork fore grips and foam butt grips. The rationale is that foam is more durable and since I am not touching the butt when fishing it makes sense to use the less expensive, tougher material for the butt.

Reels

The reel is a very important part of your fishing outfit when tossing spinners. When fly-fishing, the reel is mostly used to store line. If you are drifting with casting or spinning tackle you cast your offering, let it drift with the current and then reel the bait or lure back in at the end of the drift. When casting and retrieving spinners and other lures, you are actively using the reel to fish all the time. Whether you choose to fish with a spinning or casting reel it's critical that it is durable and works smoothly. A fast retrieve ratio and large-diameter spool are very helpful when retrieving with the current. These features also help you keep up with fast-moving steelhead, salmon, or trout.

I would like recommend reels but I have almost no experience with models currently available. Swedish-made Cardinal spinning reels have been virtually the only reels hanging on my spinning rods since the 1970s. These reels operate in an extremely smooth fashion and, since I am still using the models I started with, are obviously very durable. They came in four sizes and I use the Cardinal 3 for trout fishing, the 4 for steelhead fishing and the 6 for salmon and for steelhead in big rivers. An American company, American Classic Sales, produced a slightly improved replica of the original Cardinal 4 called the American Classic IV. Unfortunately they have ceased making these reels and the original Cardinals went out of production in the early 1980s. The reason for relating all this is that these reels still show up on the on line auction sites and if you can find one in good shape it will be worth the investment.

I'm sure there are other quality reels available today. As already emphasized the key is choosing one that operates very smoothly so that it doesn't dampen your ability to feel the spinner working. The bail system needs to be durable as you will be making lots of casts.

As promised, I am now going to make my case for using spinning reels when tossing hardware in rivers and streams. Level-wind bait-casting reels are great for making long, accurate casts and that is why they are preferred by anglers fishing the large, broad rivers of the Pacific Northwest for salmon and steelhead. However, it takes a strong swing of the rod and a fairly heavy lure to overcome inertia and get the spool revolving which means you are handicapped when making the short casts with lighter lures that are often required in smaller rivers. Even in large streams you often need to make accurate, short casts into cover along the edges and logjams and big boulders in mid stream. The spinning reel is really well suited for this finesse casting, as the line comes off the properly filled fixed spool with ease. The amount of line retrieved with each turn of the

Strong line is needed when battling big steelhead in tight quarters.

handle is usually greater with a spinning reel owing to its large spool diameter and high retrieve ratio. There is also a comfort factor. My spinning outfits are perfectly balanced with my hand just in front of the reel while a bait-caster is always top heavy with your hand below the reel. Finally, the spinning outfit is perfect for the most accurate presentation, the underhand pendulum cast, which we will describe later in this chapter.

Line

There are a myriad of lines on the market and choosing a line can get complicated. For most river spinner-fishing situations I believe nylon monofilament is the best type of line to use. The super braids and fused lines made of gel spun polyethylene can be useful in some large rivers but I have only used mono in the last ten years. Most of the time you will want to pick a very castable line because that is what you are doing a lot of when fishing with spinners. Trilene XL is my personal favorite but there are many other options on the market. The properties you want are small diameter and limpness. This allows you to fish effectively with surprisingly high-pound-test line that makes landing big trout and salmon in a snaggy river possible. Normal ultralight spinning tackle calls for two-or four-pound test but you can move up to six- and eight-pound test when spinner-fishing for trout. Obviously this is overkill when fishing for ten-inch trout but when that five-pound lunker grabs your spinner and heads for the logs you will be glad you have eight-pound test on your reel.

For steelhead and salmon you can move up to 12- to 17-pound test. The fish won't notice the line when watching the flashing spinner.

For big rivers you might want to pick a low-stretch monofilament line so that you can still set the hook when the fish hits immediately after a long cast. If the water you will be fishing has lots of rocks or other abrasive cover you may want to sacrifice some castability and pick a more abrasion-resistant line.

Since you are making lots of casts and retrieves you will be working the line hard. Thus it is very important that you change your line fairly often. Line is relatively cheap but even if it wasn't you will still want strong line that is in good shape attached to your spinner when that trophy steelhead grabs your lure. It is definitely not necessary to change all the line on the spool. I routinely just change the top 50 yards of "working line" on my steelhead and salmon reels and the top 35 yards on my trout spools. The deeper line almost never leaves the spool so why change it each time. The backing is still there if a large fish takes out lots of line. A blood knot is used to attach the new line to your "backing". Trim the knot well and place it just under the lip of the spool when reeling on the new line. This way it will not catch the line when you make a long cast.

Loading Your Vest or Tackle Box

A supply of spinners is your obvious primary need when you hit the river chasing trout, salmon, or steelhead, but there are other items that help you be successful and enjoy your outing. A vest or some kind of tackle pack that you can wear is the way to go when you are wading. While a tackle box or boxes makes sense in a boat I still wear a vest when floating in a personal watercraft or small boat as I am often out of the craft when fishing.

As you load your fishing vest, your goal is to have everything you will need for the outing on the river. Fishing time is precious and you do not want to spend it returning to your vehicle to get something you forgot or something to repair tackle. You also want to be prepared for changing water conditions, the weather, biting insects, minor mishaps, and anything else that might affect your fishing. Having the right items for the fish and conditions as well as the fix-it materials you will need if something breaks down or leaks, will make your day on the water an enjoyable and productive one. Of course you cannot carry the kitchen sink,

Lynda Hayslette wearing fully loaded vest hoists a summer-run steelhead.

so you also have to be selective and not carry all the tackle you own.

Terminal gear is obviously a very important part of the tackle you stow in your vest. Luckily it's simpler for the spinner-tosser in that you don't have to carry sinkers, hooks, swivels, leaders, and floats like the drift angler does. Basically you just need a couple of small boxes of spinners, maybe three dozen all together. I also carry a box of alternative lures, plugs and spoons, for special situations which will be discussed in a separate chapter. We will also describe in a later chapter which spinners should be in your vest based on river conditions as well as the species you are targeting.

Tools that should be in your vest include a hook sharpener, needlenose pliers, line clippers, scissors, reel wrench and screwdriver. A hook sharpener allows you to touch up those hook points dulled by the rocks.

My favorite is the thumb file with a hole in it so it can be attached to a "D" ring and be secure from being dropped in the river. A "File Saver" pouch impregnated with WD-40 will prevent rust and also keep the file from wearing a hole in your vest pocket. Needlenose pliers are handy for realigning bent hooks, flattening barbs and unhooking trout and salmon. Hemostats may also be used for unhooking fish and at times are superior to pliers—more on unhooking fish in the Landing and Releasing chapter.

Line clippers and scissors come in handy for cutting line and trimming knots. Clippers work best for monofilament and I keep one hanging from a "D" ring for quick access. Childrens' scissors, with the rounded points that won't poke holes in your vest pockets, are ideal for cutting braided line. A reel wrench and screwdriver are take-down tools for your reel. I also carry spare bail springs, which are the most likely parts to fail on my spinning reels. A small bottle of oil is carried to keep the reel running smoothly. Interestingly, the oil I have found to work best is synthetic automobile motor oil because its viscosity doesn't change with air temperature. And, even though I'm using the silkiest, most dependable reels ever built, the original Swedish Cardinals, I still carry a spare reel. You never know when you might get sand in the reel or dunk it in the river in below-freezing weather.

The extra reel can be placed in the big pocket in the back of your vest but I prefer to stash the cased reel in the large pouch created by my wader belt. When a bail spring does break I usually switch to the spare reel rather than changing the spring on the water. Of course, if something goes wrong with the spare reel, you have a third backup in the extra bail springs. I also carry two extra spools, one loaded with slightly heavier line and the other with lighter line. The spare reel will have line of the same test I've chosen for the outing. You can switch to the lighter or heavier line if conditions change or the fish composition changes. For example, the sun might come out and you might need to fish with smaller spinners so you switch to the lighter line. Or, when trout fishing you discover some summer steelhead have entered the stream and you beef up your tackle to give yourself a chance to land the larger fish.

While it is possible to stow a pack rod in the back of your vest, I usually leave my spare rod in the car. I do carry extra tip tops, guides, ferrule cement, matches, and a small roll of electrical tape for rod repair. On a memorable outing several springs ago the steelies were

pounding my spinners. The sixth fish went between my legs and I did something stupid. Rather than stepping over the line I tried to pull the fairly tired fish back up. With the rod pointed away from the fish, the angle was too sharp and the rod sounded like a rifle shot as the tip section snapped about two feet from the tip. I still landed the steelhead but I was two miles from the spotted vehicle and figured it would be at least an hour round-trip hike. I overlapped the broken pieces with the uppermost on the underside of the rod and liberally wrapped them in electrical tape. It wasn't pretty but I landed eight more steelhead as I fished my way upstream to the car.

I always keep polarized sunglasses in a case in my vest. While I am usually wearing them, it's good to have a place to stow them if you are fishing until dark and to know that they will be there for your next outing. A small first-aid/personal-comfort kit in a resealable plastic bag is easy to stow and can make your day on the river more pleasant. Mine includes lip balm, Band Aids, aspirin, toilet paper and, during the month of June, antihistamines for my grass pollen allergy. A small plastic bottle of insect repellent should be carried during spring and summer if mosquitoes or black flies are present. I minimize the surface area exposed by wearing a lightweight, tightly woven nylon long-sleeved shirt. Water and some high-energy food are also important when making a long wade or float. Freezing water in a plastic bottle, keeping it in the wader pocket, and drinking it as it thaws works well. Candy and granola bars are easy to pack for energy. Another plan, which I have been employing in recent years, is to carry celery and carrot sticks in a plastic bag. These veggies supply both sustenance and water. Usually I also add grapes to the mix. Bananas and apples also work well for these tasks.

The large pouch in the back of your vest is a good place to store a compact wading rain jacket. If it's cool or cloudy and threatening to rain, I just wear the jacket. But if the weather changes and the sun makes an appearance it makes sense to stow the jacket in order to keep you from getting wet from sweating. Speaking of staying dry, it's important to have a wader-patching kit in your vest. We will go into greater detail on wader care and patching in the wading techniques chapter.

Additional items that I carry, but are optional include a pen and some cards to record river conditions and the location and size of fish caught. I often use the backs of old, out-of-date business cards. Several are kept in the small plastic "wallets" that are often given out when you purchase your fishing license. While often the size of the fish is just estimated, a DeLiar type scale and tape is carried to measure exceptional specimens before release. Water temperatures are taken with a bi-metallic type pocket thermometer and recorded. Usually just the start and end temperatures are noted but sometimes intermediate temperature might be important. While I normally stay with the stream, there will be times when cutting cross-country is the plan and a compass will keep you on track. A small flashlight will help you stay on the trail to the car if the fishing is so good it keeps you on the river after sunset.

A camera will be an optional item for most anglers but as an outdoor writer it's an especially important item for me. In my opinion, we could easily make a case for the importance of having a camera in the vest or on the boat for all river anglers. It allows you to record many great memories by capturing action shots and photographing fish when they are freshly landed and still alive. "Having proof" makes it a lot easier to release those trophy steelhead, trout and salmon. Compact, point-and-shoot digital cameras are ideal but even one-time-use film cameras take surprisingly good photos when there is ample light. A reclosable plastic bag will protect the camera when not in use and a long strap that you can put around your neck will keep you from accidentally dropping the camera in the river when shooting. Of course, you can always buy a waterproof model and not have to sweat an accidental dunking.

There is an infinite variety of vests and tackle packs on the market. Pick one with pockets big enough to hold your largest items and enough pockets to keep things organized. If you are a year-round salmonid chaser you will want two. A lightweight mesh type for the summer trout fishing and one of larger capacity for cooler weather and anadromous fish. While cotton is comfortable it's not very durable so I suggest one made of nylon or a polyester blend for longer life.

Spinner-fishing Techniques

'Slow' is the key word when casting and retrieving weighted spinners. It's important to take advantage of the spinner's ability to have action or spin at a slow rate of retrieve. The longer you keep the lure in the strike zone the more effective it will be. And, a slowly spinning blade is more effective than one that is whirring at a blurring speed.

When casting upstream or quartering upstream you need to retrieve your lure just enough faster than the current to keep it spinning. This may seem too fast for the fish when the current is really ripping but remember trout and salmon are also in this quick flow and can catch up with your spinner quite easily. Casting across stream or quartering downstream and sweeping your spinner across the current is a very effective technique and should be employed whenever you can get alongside or above the fish-holding location without alerting the trout, salmon, or steelhead of your presence.

When sweeping your spinner across the current you need to retrieve only enough line to keep the blade turning on your lure. If quartering downstream you may not have to reel at all. When the spinner gets directly below you it will tend to rise due to its resistance to the flow. You can keep it down and extend your presentation by slowly giving line at a rate slower than the current which keeps the blade turning as it continues down through the holding water. Your overall spinner-fishing goal is to keep the blade slowly turning through as much good holding water as possible for migrating anadromous salmon and steelhead or feeding trout. We will describe the best holding water and how to fish the various types in a later chapter.

Casting accuracy is an important component of river fishing for trout and salmon because the closer you present your spinner to the fish the more-hook ups you will have. The compactness of the weighted spinner makes it easy to cast and you need to take advantage of this. The conventional overhead and side-arm casts do the job in large streams, but when you really want to get close to the cover you should employ the underhand, pendulum cast. It's the only cast to use in small streams and creeks and it will allow you to get your spinner close to the cover-hugging fish in larger rivers.

The underhand cast is accomplished by letting your spinner hang about four feet below your rod tip. The spinner is swung back in a pendulum motion to load the rod and then rapidly swung forward and released. This is similar to the lob cast a bait-angler might make except that with major wrist action you line-drive the spinner to its target.

A major plus for this cast is that you always have your lure in sight. It also travels in a low trajectory over the water so that you can cast underneath overhanging trees and other vegetation. And, obviously, you don't worry about obstructions behind and above you or to the side like you do with overhead and sidearm casts. Since you are watching your lure head for your target you can make mid-air corrections by moving the rod and slowing or stopping the lure's progress.

No weights or leaders necessary

Rigging

Rigging up for spinner-fishing is extremely simple. Unlike fly and drift fishing there are no leaders, sinkers, and swivels involved. You simply tie on your spinner and start casting. Some will argue that you need a swivel to prevent line twist, but I don't think it's necessary, and that its presence detracts from the spinner.

A spinner does temporarily twist your line but as long as it does not just spin continuously in one direction line twist will not build up and cause problems. In river fishing, the blade on your spinner will usually bump a rock or the bottom on most casts. Each time this happens the torque developed in the line by the spinning blade will cause the spinner blade to spin in the opposite direction when it starts again. If you are fishing deep water with sweep casts you can get the spinner blade to change direction by giving it momentary slack to stop the blade from spinning and then starting again. After a long downstream sweep you should start and stop your retrieve several times as you reel your spinner back in for the next cast to keep line twist from building up. As final insurance against built-up line twist, lift your spinner from the water with six or more feet of line out at the end of the retrieve and allow the lure to spin to remove any twist in your line before the next cast. If you still feel

the need for a swivel, use a small black one. You can also incorporate one in your home built spinner when building them (see Chapter 10).

My usual knot for tying on the lure is the Trilene knot but the improved clinch knot will also work well. You want a knot that is strong but not one that is 100% and these knots break at about 90% of the line strength. The reason is that when it becomes necessary to break off a snagged spinner you want the line to break right at the lure and not leave a bunch of line in the river. This involves technique and we will talk more about getting unsnagged in a later chapter.

When you tie on a spinner it's important that you lubricate the line with water or saliva and pull the knot together slowly. Then, really test the knot severely to make sure it is a good one, and periodically recheck the knot as you fish. Also check the line near the knot for abrasions. I routinely retie my spinner after each fish, as well as when I notice some abrasion near the knot. Obviously you will be retying when you check your knot and it breaks. You absolutely don't want a trophy trout or steelhead to find a bad knot or frayed line for you.

In recent years I have added an item to my terminal tackle when fishing with spinners. A small, black Duo-Lock snap is tied to the end of my line most of the time. A #2 is employed when fishing for steelhead and salmon and a #1 or #2 is used for trout. The reason is that it allows me to easily change spinners if the conditions tell me a different lure will be better. If we have to cut and retie we often decide not to bother but if the switch is easy we will put the better spinner on the end of our line. The next chapter is all about picking the right spinner for what you find around the next bend in the stream.

Trilene Knot

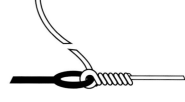

CHAPTER 3

Matching the Conditions

The weighted spinner could be considered a foreign object in the river. It really doesn't resemble any living creature. A case can be made that the flash of the blade is similar, at least momentarily, to the flash of a smolt, shiner or other baitfish. Or, perhaps when fished near the bottom, a brass-bladed model faintly resembles a crayfish.

When resident trout are feeding they will still utilize cover most of the time to keep themselves from

Terri Bedford used the "right" spinner to hook this steelhead.

being eaten and to hide from prey they hope to ambush. I think that a spinner looks alive and arouses the curiosity of trout. It usually represents a larger food item to the trout, especially when they are feeding on aquatic insect nymphs. Fish know innately that they need to take in more calories than they expend and the spinner probably appears to be a "good meal". Thus, it's "worth it" to them to leave their cover and grab the lure.

When steelhead, salmon and other anadromous salmonids leave the ocean or large lake and enter their natal or stocked stream, their primary goal is to travel to their spawning grounds and then procreate when ready. Migrating steelhead, cutthroat trout, Atlantic salmon, and brown trout retain the ability to feed but rarely do so actively. Our five species of Pacific salmon become unable to swallow and digest food once they enter the river. The instinct or memory to feed is still there and they will opportunistically pick up food items on their river migration. Another instinct remains present and dates back to their early river life when they were growing to smolt size. That trait is territorialism and you can bet these fish will still defend their "space" when they return to the river.

Migrating salmonids will also be adjusting to a much shallower environment when they move up the tributaries. They feel more vulnerable and seek cover as they travel. We must take this wariness/shyness into consideration when we fish for them.

While there will be some appeal to their feeding instinct, when we fish with spinners or other artificial lures and flies for anadromous trout and salmon, we are primarily invading their territory with the hope that they will attack the intruder. It would seem that something large and gaudy would always be a good choice but we must remember these fish are now in a new, relatively shallow environment and it's definitely possible to spook them with a lure that is too big or flashy. Similarly it's possible to scare a resident rainbow or brown back into its hide out with a spinner that is too large or bright.

The goal with all trout and salmon is to get their attention and evoke a positive response. To do this we must match the river and atmospheric conditions with a lure that makes them mad or curious or want to eat but does not spook them. For this discussion we are going to use the weighted spinner with French type blades as an example because they are usually the best choice when fishing rivers. But we will also touch on matching the other lures to the conditions.

As ardent stream anglers we may fish a small, ultra-clear stream on a sunny day or a large river with water visibility measured in inches on a dark, rainy day, and everything in between.

Muddiness or turbidity blocks out light and decreases lateral visibility. It's usually caused by suspended sediments from runoff or high water mobilizing the stream-bottom sand and silt. Plankton can also cause turbidity, especially in rivers with impoundments on them. Rivers can also be stained with tannic acids or other compounds that decrease light penetration but still allow trout and salmon to see well laterally because the water is clear but colored. Checking visibility or clarity of the river is the first thing I do when I arrive. When the stream is reasonably clear you can do this by simply seeing how deep you can see the bottom. For more turbid conditions I use my net rim and lightcolored wading staff. If my net rim disappears in less than one foot of depth I generally won't fish with lures unless it's a small creek that I know really well. From one to two feet of visibility is still kind of marginal for spinners, but if the river is not too high and you can still read the water well you can fish your lures with confidence. As clarity increases to three feet your options increase greatly as the steelhead and trout can see most moving lures in time to nail them. The coveted steelhead-green occurs with four to five of visibility and is prime for fishing lures.

Make the gravel bottom start to get fuzzy at four feet and all steelheaders start to drool. Slight turbidity or stain also helps resident trout feel like they can venture out safely while still being able to see their prey well. I like to think of this as the river having just the right mystery in the holding water. More than six feet of visibility is considered clear to ultra clear, and any offering is very visible to the fish.

Let's say your chosen stream is fairly small and it's very clear when you arrive. In addition, the sun is out and shade is pretty sparse. It's time to use a small spinner, such as a #2 (using the numbering system of the Mepps Aglia series) with a nickel, brass or copper blade (see the section below on metal reflectivity). For trout you might tie on a #0 in brass or copper or a #1 in the same finishes but with blades that have tarnished a bit. If the steelhead spinner still seems too bright try a black blade or, as is my preference, a fairly tarnished copper or brass #2 blade. As the sun drops lower in the sky and you encounter a bit more shade or the holding water is deeper you might switch to a silver spinner in size 2 or a #3 gold for steelhead and salmon and a shiny #1 brass for trout.

For a steelhead outing on a medium sized stream with three to four feet of visibility you might choose a size 4 spinner with a silver blade on a cloudy day. If the sun comes out, drop down to a size 3 silver spinner or switch to a gold or brass #4. On a larger, more turbid river it's time to choose the gaudiest spinners you have in your vest. Number 5 or 6 spinners with matte silver blades, bright fluorescent bodies, and tape on the back of their blades are the ones to try. For trout in larger rivers I rarely go larger than spinners with #2 blades, but you can switch to real silver for more visibility.

Even when you're on the same river be ready to adapt your lure to the changing water and atmospheric conditions that you encounter as you are fishing. Deep, well-shaded runs require large spinners and relatively shallow tailouts that are open to the sky require significant downsizing. Riffled surfaces decrease light penetration so use somewhat larger, brighter spinners here than when there is glassy-smooth surface over the same-depth water. These are just a few examples of the water types and conditions to consider when choosing your lure. One word of caution, don't get too hung up on having the perfect size and blade finish for the water you are fishing so that you are spending too much time changing lures. Pick one that fits most of the holding water and conditions and fish it hard. Change only when there is a really significant change, such as entering a canyon, a stretch of much shallower or deeper water, it starts to rain and both the sky and the water get darker, etc.

Some anglers in the Northwest believe water temperature should play a role in your spinner selection, with larger lures for colder water. In my 40-plus years of hard-core spinner-fishing for steelhead and salmon I have not found this to be true. In fact, when the water is at 35 degrees or less, the opposite may be true. In recent years my success in Michigan's rather large Grand River has increased by downsizing my spinners in winter when the water is often at 32 degrees or even super cooled a bit lower. I think Pacific Northwest anglers that believe in larger lures for low river temperatures are really matching the darker conditions of winter with the sun lower in the sky and typical rainy, cloudy weather with higher, more turbid flows. Similarly the theory for small, duller spinners for summer-runs matches the low clear water and high sun of summer.

In addition to matching the conditions with the size and finish of your spinner you should also modify your technique as the visibility decreases. Upstream casts are only effective when there is ample visibility and trout and salmon can see the spinner in time to intercept it. As the water becomes more turbid it's important to slow your presentation and increase the time the lure is spinning near the fish. So more across-stream casts should be made as the visibility decreases. Eventually you will be concentrating your casts quartering downstream so the spinners hang in front of the fish. This is always an effective cast but it becomes essential when visibility drops to less than two feet. Luckily, this increase in turbidity allows you to get above the fish, even in very small streams, without spooking them.

Often fish will help you match conditions with the right spinner. If you are not seeing any interest and you know salmon, steelhead, or trout are present it may be that your spinner is too small and isn't getting their attention. Conversely, if the fish follow but don't hit or come after the spinner and then flare away, the spinner may be too bright or gaudy.

There is a final piece of advice as you try to match conditions with your chosen technique. It's usually best to err on the side of too small rather than too large and gaudy. Using the smallest spinner that can be cast far enough, get down to the fish in their holding area, attract their attention and elicit a strike has worked best for me.

A silver spinner fools coho.

Metal Reflectivity

The amount of light a metal finish reflects is a really complicated subject. Light is made up of many wavelengths which correspond to many colors. The wavelengths that are absorbed versus those that are reflected determine the color of an object. White reflects all light, while black absorbs all wavelengths. A green lure reflects the green wavelengths and absorbs enough of the others so that it looks green.

The amount of light a metal surface reflects is partly dependant on the kind of light that strikes it. For example, some surfaces reflect relatively more light under low-light conditions at dusk or on a cloudy day. The quality of the metal surface also plays a role. Because of all the variables, we are going to generalize and give approximate values as we describe the various metals used for spinner blades, spoons, and other metallic lures.

Silver reflects the most light, something over 90%, and gives a very white flash because it's reflecting most of the wavelengths of light. Gold is next in line, reflecting a percentage of light in the mid 80's. It obviously best reflects yellow wavelengths giving it the color flash it has. Copper and brass, which is a copper and zinc alloy, generally reflect between 70

and 80 percent of the light that strikes their surface. Nickel and chromium are at the bottom of the list in their ability to reflect light, generally around 60% or less. Their flash is rather dark too because they are bouncing back a lesser amount of light. It's interesting that many anglers describe the brightest steelhead as "chromers" because in actuality the name doesn't do them justice. Their shiny flanks are way brighter than any chrome plate.

Nickel is a very popular finish because it looks good in the store and never tarnishes. Its mirror finish turns out to be a negative on a dark steelhead or trout stream, as it reflects its surroundings. Even though silver bounces back lots of light, a shiny silver plate can also be mirror-like and not show up well in a well-shaded stream. I always use silver blades with a matte or frosty finish for my steelhead and salmon spinners. Gold has the advantage of never tarnishing and is a great finish for sunny days. Copper and brass are also good finishes when visibility is good. While they tarnish quite readily, they are easily polished back to their original shine and tarnished blades can be very effective in clear water on bright days. In fact, I always let some of my brass and copper spinners tarnish naturally and keep them in my spinner box for just such conditions.

CHAPTER 4

Reading & Covering Water

As previously mentioned, the weighted spinner is a real attention-getter, both visibly and sonically. It has what I like to call a large cylinder of attraction as it travels through water. Depending on clarity of the water it can attract strikes from trout, salmon, and steelhead from a distance of ten feet or more. A fly imitating a nymph that fish are feeding on or salmon eggs are probably more likely to attract a take than a spinner, but their cylinder of attraction is much smaller. Thus it takes more casts to cover the holding water with bait and exact imitations of food. To be successful with spinners it's important to become adept at reading water and then covering lots of possible feeding or resting stations on each outing. Spinner-fishing could also be described as "aerobic angling" because you are constantly on the move. However, to effectively cover lots of water you must be able to read the water well and we'll start there.

Decoding the River

One of the reasons river and creek fishing is so appealing to me is that you are able to figure out where fish will be by using your own senses. Except, perhaps, for very large, deep rivers you don't need a depth finder, fish locator, underwater camera, dissolved oxygen probe, pH meter, or other electronic gadget to tell you where to present your lure.

There will be times when experience and intuition are relied upon when searching for salmon, steelhead, and trout, but vision remains the key sense when decoding a river for the location of its silver visitor or resident trout. You will also use your sense of feel a lot when spinner-fishing. On occasion you will even hear a fish that you don't see because you were looking in another direction. Just a few weeks prior to writing this section I was having no luck fishing for steelhead in Michigan's Grand River when I heard a big splash. I looked in the direction of the noise, saw the surface disturbance, made a cast just upstream of it, and was soon hooked up to my only silver bullet of the outing. I even have a friend that swears he can smell steelhead. This is probably more a case of finding water that looks perfect for holding steelhead, reeks of steelhead if you will, than actually smelling the fish. However, I think I have smelled steelhead in small streams on several occasions, usually in summer. Obviously, knowing something about the biology and habits of fish is also important in finding and hooking the treasures in our streams. We will go into depth on the biology of these fish in separate chapters.

Cover seems to be especially important to migrating salmon and steelhead. They have just left the vastness and depths of the ocean or Great Lake so it's easy to see how they might feel vulnerable in their new, much shallower river environment. Anadromous fish are on the move and tend to align themselves with the main current. As they make their way upstream the fish will also be searching for resting places in or near the main flow of the river. Thus, when you find obstacles in the major flow that both block the current and offer overhead protection, you have located an ideal holding spot for migrating salmon and steelhead.

When anadromous fish have traveled through a long, shallow rapid area they will look for the first resting spot they can find. This is usually in the tailout of the next deep run or pool. As soon as there is enough depth and cover for the fish to feel safe they will "take

A boulder garden provides cover and resting areas.

a break" from their migration. Any boulders, logs, or rock and clay ledges in this area should be fished very hard when steelhead and salmon are on the move.

The upper or head ends of holes or pools also deserve lots of attention. It is here that steelhead lie just before they attempt to travel through the next stretch of shallow water. These fish are often anxious to move on and can be very aggressive. The broken surfaces from upstream riffles or rapids provide protection and often continue into the top of the pool. Salmon and steelhead often lie within a few feet of the lip of the shallow bar. Keep your rod tip up when you cast your spinner into the riffle and when you reach the edge drop it to help the spinner get down quickly to the fish.

Slots are created in areas where the main current intersects with backeddies caused by "friction" of the water movement interacting with an irregular bank or one with lots of root wads, logs or other cover next to it. Steelhead are often concentrated in slots because of their desire to be in or near fast current yet not have to fight it. These narrow, quiet-water areas are perfect resting spots for steelhead and salmon so make lots of presentations to them. They also make a perfect spot for trout to intercept food items drifting with the current.

Sometimes you'll find be long reaches without slots or the classic "riffle, pool, and tailout" configuration. If these areas do not contain any boulders, logs or other obstructions they may not hold very many, or any, fish. Look for any surface disturbance that would indicate deeply submerged boulders or other cover.

An otter also thinks this is good woody cover for trout.

Make sweep-casts with your spinner and try to detect the presence of deep cover by either ticking it with the blade or feeling a change in current speed. Even if you don't find any submerged cover, if the current strength feels right you should still cover the area.

Choppy surfaces of riffles often provide the best protection or cover for migrating steelhead and salmon when rivers are low and very clear. This is especially true for summer steelhead. In clear water you can often spot steelhead in fairly deep water if the surface is glassy smooth. And if you can see the fish, it can see you. These same gray torpedoes that are very visible in six feet of water can disappear in a choppy riffle that is half that depth or less.

It's a popular belief among steelhead and trout anglers that higher levels of dissolved oxygen are present in riffles and this attracts fish, especially steelhead in summertime. In most trout and steelhead streams this is simply not the case. The dissolved oxygen is at or near saturation throughout the stream—slow pools and riffles alike. The fact that the real reason summer steelhead lie in deep riffles is for cover rather than dissolved oxygen is probably moot to most anglers, but knowing they are there for protection will help you fish them better.

Resident trout are also very cover oriented, especially older, larger browns, brookies, rainbows and cutts. In large streams and those with water that's naturally

stained or turbid, water depth alone provides trout with cover. However, most trout streams are usually clear and you will find that large trout prefer something more solid, such as a big log, logjam, or overhanging vegetation. Depth becomes less and less important the better the overhead cover. This is especially true in Eastern and Midwestern streams. Many, many times a big brown has slid out from heavy cover in less than a foot of water to grab my spinner.

Unlike salmon and steelhead, stream trout need to feed. Drifting insects and other aquatic invertebrates are more concentrated in shallow, fast flows and trout can feed more efficiently in shallow water. While trout rest and hide in deep pools or under heavy cover out of the current, they will often move to shallower water to intercept drifting food items. Thus it is important to look hard for any cover in shallow water that might provide protection for feeding trout and fish it well.

Usually large trout try to keep their feeding stations close to their sanctuary so they can quickly return to safety if they sense danger. Small beds of watercress or other aquatic vegetation, an overhanging bush, grass or tree branch dragging in the water, or similar cover should receive special attention when found just above or alongside a big hole.

When excellent cover is found in combination with a good feeding lane you have the perfect situation. Look for areas where logs or rocks concentrate the flow of the stream and funnel food. Undercut banks are especially great places to find large feeding trout because a major portion of the food-laden flow actually goes under the cover letting the trout dine in total seclusion. Retrieving your spinner along the edge of the undercut is a great way to draw the trout out for a bigger meal.

Always keep in mind that riffles are the food factories of our trout creeks and rivers. The rocky, uneven bottom provides the cracks and crevices that are great habitat for many species of insects, crustaceans, and other invertebrates, as well as small fish like darters and sculpins. Watch for cover in and just downstream from cobbly riffles and fish it hard. Remember that a riffled surface also provides cover, both feeding trout and migrating steelhead hug the bottom of deep riffles even when no additional cover is present.

Polarized sunglasses are an essential part of reading and fishing rivers for trout and anadromous salmonids. They decrease surface glare so you can spot underwater cover and current blockers. In most cases choose the lightest-tinted lenses that are still 100% polarized.

Stream corridors are pretty dark, especially when well shaded by large trees or when flowing through canyons. You want to maximize the amount of light passing through while still cutting as much surface glare as possible. Amber is the first choice for me. Check to see if the glasses are 100% polarized by taking two pair of the same kind and rotating the lenses 90 degrees to each other as you look through them. They should go dark and opaque if they are completely polarized.

Sometimes you will find fishy looking water that's hard to read and doesn't have any obvious covers or slots. Look for subtle differences in the otherwise nondescript water. A good example is an almost-never-fail long bend on Michigan's Pere Marquette River. The current and depth were ideal for winter steelhead but there weren't any logs or other significant cover. But, in one spot a small branch just touched the water and rippled the river surface slightly. I caught steelhead with regularity in this bend and every one was hooked under that branch.

Another hint for relatively non-descript water is to look for foam or bubbles on the surface. The areas where they are most concentrated are also likely where the main flow is located. So, if you are at a loss as to where to cast, fish under the bubbles.

Moving Right Along

As mentioned at the beginning of this chapter, it's important to take advantage of the spinner's attraction power and cover lots of water on each outing. We will concentrate on hiking and wading here, and save floating for a separate chapter. Fishing from bridge to bridge or access site to access site without having to walk back to your vehicle is the best plan. This is accomplished by fishing with a partner or partners. One angler or pair is dropped off at their start bridge or access point and the vehicle is driven to their get-out point, where the second angler or pair starts their fishing. The lower angler fishes to the vehicle and then drives to pick up his or her partner(s) at their get-out point. This works especially well when there are bridges about equidistant apart, but also can be accomplished when a road approximately parallels a stream. When there is no defined midpoint, the upstream angler can tie fluorescent tape to an overhanging branch to indicate where he started and the vehicle is parked.

Covering lots of stream allowed Lynda Hayslette to find this steelhead.

If you are fishing on your own you should still strive to wade/walk a considerable stretch of water. Depending on the stream and terrain, you may be able to cut off loops or take other shortcuts on your way back. Or if the best route is to just follow the stream, you can give some especially good-looking spots a second try. And, if you miss a fish on the way up, there's a good chance that after a long rest it will hit again when you return downstream.

Even though the most effective cast with a spinner is the down-and-across sweep, moving in an upstream direction is the best plan. This is especially true in small and medium-sized streams. Resident trout are very wary and even steelhead and salmon are much less likely to strike your lure if they know you are there. Anglers using bait can sometimes get away with betraying their presence, but a steelhead is unlikely to grab an unnatural lure like a spinner if you have been busted.

All trout and salmon face into the current unless chasing prey or migrating. It's their nature to look forward and up, so it's to our advantage to move upstream. Moving slowly and keeping a low profile are also important. Even though they are looking upstream, a quick movement by a large predator in waders behind them will still likely send fish into the closest cover.

While not as often a problem in high-gradient western streams, moving upstream also prevents sand and silt from being stirred up and sent downstream, betraying your presence. In addition, it helps keep sounds you make wading from being transmitted to the fish.

*Nick Amato casts a spinner
into a slot by a huge rock.*

The ripples or wake you send out when wading are also not as likely to reach and alarm trout and steelhead.

So how do we make the magical quartering down cast and resultant sweep across the holding water while moving upstream? Well, we cautiously work upstream and plan ahead on how we will fish each holding area as we come to it. We can still cast our spinner upstream and retrieve it downstream at a speed slightly faster than the current so it will spin slowly. With wily resident trout this may be the only option and is still a great way to catch them.

As you sneak upstream look for ways to make a sweep presentation unnoticed. If a log goes across stream I slowly and quietly wade up along the edge of the creek. Staying below the log I cast across and extending my rod upstream above the log sweeps the spinner in front of and just under the log. The log helps keep the steelhead or trout lying under it from seeing you, but if you had moved downstream of the log it would not help to block you.

Utilize this technique whenever the cover that is hiding the fish also helps hide you. This can be overhanging vegetation, an undercut bank, large rock, or a rock or clay ledge. Water depth, turbidity, and a broken surface can also help you sneak alongside and above holding water.

Something to be alert for when you are wading up to get in position are back eddies, especially when silt or fine sand is present. It doesn't do much good to be quiet and slow moving when you are stirring up the bottom

and it's moving upstream ahead of you and circling into the holding water. Sometimes it's best to get on the bank and circle upstream of the holding water. It's a bit more difficult to stay out of sight since you are higher so I usually try to stay in the water. But, by cutting back away from the stream you can avoid detection on the bank. Fish seem especially sensitive to vibrations produced by footfall on the bank and transmitted to the water, so walk slowly and lightly. Usually it's best to kneel on the bank when you reach your casting position.

In addition to avoiding eddies, pay attention to the substrate where you are wading. Try to avoid areas with loose rock and gravel that will shift, grind together, and make noise when you walk on them. Often the best path is through somewhat deeper, slower water. There will be less current to fight and you will be better able to stay out of sight when you are waist deep in the stream.

How fast to fish the water is always in question. Lots of factors must be taken into consideration: Water clarity, stream size, water depth, amount of cover, and the confidence you have in a spot all influence the number of casts to make before moving on. It's often said that if a steelhead is going to hit a lure it will happen on the first cast and retrieve that passes near it. While I agree that both anadromous fish and resident trout usually say 'yea or nay' early on with a flashing spinner, I have a two-cast-minimum rule. You might make the perfect cast to a holding fish but the trout or steelhead may not see it in time or be prepared to grab it. To put it in human terms, they may think "what was that that just flashed by" and let it go, even though they might be inclined to eat or attack it. On the second cast they are ready to nail the spinner when it first comes into view.

The more confidence you have in a spot, the more presentations you should make. Naturally, if the holding water is expansive and water visibility is reduced by turbidity it will take quite a few casts to make sure any holding fish have seen your spinner. Conversely, if the water is very clear and the stream or holding spot is small, two good casts should be all that are needed.

As an example, let's fish a deep riffle with a large boulder in the center of it. You found the boulder by either seeing a bulge in the surface, ticking it with your spinner blade, or feeling a reduction in the current or a soft spot in front of it as your spinner swept across the flow. The water is quite clear but there is enough turbidity to the water that, combined with the riffled surface, keeps you from seeing the bottom.

Side View

Top View

Dürten Kampmann

Dürten Kampmann

Fish holding in a deep riffle with a large boulder.

The large boulder creates three prime lies: Below the rock, fish will hold in the slots formed below each side of the boulder. These current dead spots are formed where the backeddy behind the boulder intersects with the main current flow on each side of the boulder. The prime spot, in my opinion, is located just upstream of the rock. The dominant stream trout will be here, where it gets the first crack at drifting food morsels. The most active steelhead and salmon lie above the boulder getting ready to continue their journey upstream. Focus on these soft spots in the current by feel and make several sweeps behind the rock at varying distances from the rock. Then repeat above the rock, making a few extra casts because it's the most likely holding location.

While the sweep cast is most effective, whenever you are concerned about spooking fish because of the small size of the stream or clarity of the water, always make some upstream casts with downstream retrieves first. This is still an effective presentation. It requires clear water so the fish see it in time, but that's just the condition that caused you to make the upstream cast. There will also be times when the holding water is narrow and deep, making it difficult to get a sweep down to the fish. Again, this is time to make a straight upstream cast and reel in the spinner just a bit faster than the current. This will get the spinner deep but you must keep your rod tip up some and be ready to raise it when the blade ticks bottom to keep it from snagging up—a bigger hazard to upstream casts.

There is a scenario when you can skip the two-cast rule for steelhead and salmon but still keep your lure in the water. When you are wading through flat, shallow areas where you don't expect to find any fish, you can still "troll" it as you pass through. Simply wade on the side of the stream least likely to hold fish and cast across. Keep wading upstream as the spinner sweeps across. Every now and then you will be surprised by a strong yank that spins you around. These bonuses are transition fish moving to the next good holding water.

As you connect with steelhead, salmon, and stream trout, file the locations in your mind and look for similar spots on the rest of your outing. Fish these likely areas extra hard. Also remember where you caught fish when you try a new river. The parameters that make good holding water for resting steelhead and feeding trout are universal. As you move upstream, always keep in mind that the current delivers food to resident trout and provides the direction for migrating anadromous visitors.

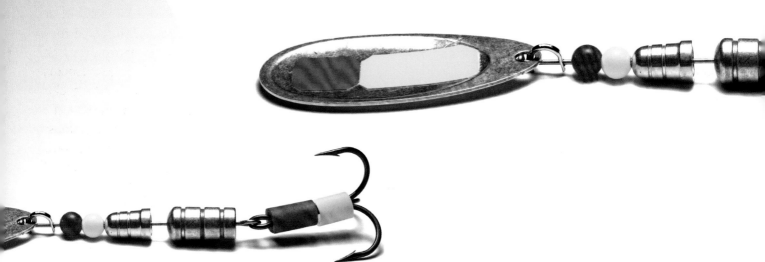

CHAPTER 5

Aggressive & Safe Wading

Spinner-fishing is a very active technique for catching steelhead, salmon, and trout. You can't stand in one spot or wade a limited area and be successful tossing these lures. We will discuss wader types, repair materials, and techniques to get you into position to catch fish while keeping you dry and safe.

Waders

The wading angler has lots of options when it comes to waders. When selecting a pair of waders it's important to consider the seasons you will be fishing and how often you will hit the stream. If you are a serious river angler and go often you will definitely need more than

Terri Bedford dons single canvas waders to catch this nice brown trout.

one pair. Just like rods and reels, you want different styles of waders to fit different river and weather conditions, and will need back-up waders if you are on a multi-day trip or fish often from your home base.

There is one style of waders that you can eliminate if you are serious about actively wading streams. Hip boots or waders are way too limiting for almost all types of water. I have never owned a pair. While you can get away with hip waders in some small streams they still keep you from fishing the stream properly in many instances. You can stay dry by walking around deep holes, but the best presentation spot is often standing in deep water. In addition, there will be times when you want to get on your knees to stay undetected. With the development of today's lightweight breathable waders the excuse that chest waders are too hot and uncomfortable is no longer valid.

Today there are basically three styles of waders: rubber- or urethane-backed nylon or canvas, breathable, and neoprene. All are available in either stocking-foot or boot-foot models. The rubber-backed nylon style is least expensive and has the advantage of being quite tough when you are trekking through thorny brush. But they don't breathe and don't stretch. Breathable waders have pretty much replaced canvas waders for cool to warm-weather fishing. While you can wear lots of layers of clothing under breathable waders, for cold-weather fishing neoprene waders continue to be my go-to boots for fishing Great Lakes tributaries in winter.

Most anglers don stocking-foot, breathable waders for the majority of their fishing. Lace-up wading shoes give your feet a lot more support than the molded boots on boot-foot waders. The obvious reason is that you have to be able to put on the boot-foot waders as is, while you can loosen the laces on the wading shoes and tighten them up to fit. Wading shoes also tend to give your feet more protection when wading and walking along rocky streams. Stocking-foot waders are also easy to dry after fishing. Even though they are breathable you will still end up with some dampness from perspiration and, of course, the neoprene booties/socks will trap moisture. To dry, simply turn them inside out, an impossibility with boot-foot waders.

The big pluses for boot-foot waders are the ease with which you can put them on and the fact that they make it much easier to keep your feet warm. My first pair of neoprene waders had stocking feet and I had lots of trouble keeping my feet warm, even with extra socks. The problem is that the water pressure can squeeze the stocking around your foot. Since air is providing most of the insulation it's easy to see why your feet get cold.

As a hardcore wading angler I have a number of waders going all the time. Both stocking-foot and boot-foot breathable waders are found in my angling closet. I wear the stocking-foots when going on long hikes/wades over rocky ground. The boot-foots are utilized for shorter, easier outings. In late fall through early spring I wear boot-foot neoprene waders. I also wear them when wading strong currents. Because they stretch, you can buy a size that hugs your lower body and legs and thus has lower water resistance.

Having good-fitting waders is important. Make sure your boots or wading shoes are fairly roomy. It's better to need an extra pair of socks than to have them too tight. Obviously, if they are too snug they may restrict circulation and result in cold feet. The legs need to be long enough and either stretch or be roomy enough so that you can step over logs and other obstacles without binding. A good test in the shop is to see if you can lift your knee above your waist without them binding. You will also want to avoid waders with too long an inseam. The extra material will increase drag in the water and rub against each leg, resulting in chafing wear that will ultimately cause leaks.

Pick the boot or wading shoe sole that gives the best traction on the rivers and during the seasons you usually fish. If you are normally fishing rocky rivers where the substrate is frequently made slippery by its coat of algae you will want felt soles. Since felt is difficult to clean and disinfect and aquatic nuisance organisms, such as the one that causes whirling disease, can be spread by hitchhiking on your boots, felt may be replaced by the time you read this. Conversely, if the stream bottom is usually silt, sand, or small gravel then boots with cleated rubber soles are the ones to wear. Cleated soles are also the best to use when there is snow on the bank. Wet felt soles are great at picking up the white stuff and soon you will be taller, but walking will be more difficult. Of course, you could use the extra height to cross a deep run, but you had better be quick.

In the wintertime in Michigan when I am fishing a rocky area, such as the rapids of the Grand River in the city of Grand Rapids, I combine rubber-soled boots with Korkers. These cleated sandals also provide good traction on ice shelves. While the snow doesn't stick to them they don't provide good traction either so I try to stay in the river. These sandals are quite heavy and don't work well for long hikes. They can also wear holes in your boots. I am hoping that if felt is phased out, studded felt soles will be replaced with studded rubber soles of some kind on wading shoes and the boots of boot-foot waders. The studs will need to be made of a durable material like carbide, and it would also be helpful if they were replaceable since even carbide wears out with heavy use.

Buy the best pair of waders you can afford. If you need to start out with an economy pair, don't fret, they will serve as a back-up pair when you upgrade. We will talk about caring for and patching your boots after we hit the river.

Wading & Wading Helpers

The stream tries to make wading difficult by hiding obstacles like submerged logs, boulders, clay and rock ledges, and an uneven or slippery substrate. Deep water and fast current can also keep you from getting to where you want to be or cause you to get wet trying. Paying attention to what is ahead and always making sure you have one foot planted securely before you move the other will keep you dry and safely moving upstream.

When wading in strong current try to keep sideways to the flow to minimize water resistance. Move with shuffle steps so that your legs never become crossed. Keep in mind that your center of gravity is between your waist and hips. Take care that the current does not cause you to lose your balance and tip you over when wading in deeper water. When crossing a swift stream try to pick a path that allows you to go both across and down so you don't have to fight the current as much as you wade to the other side.

In addition to helping you read water and find fish-holding cover your polarized sunglasses will help you spot underwater wading obstacles. Also pay attention to breaks in the surface current, they often indicate big rocks or submerged logs. When the water is off color it is important to slow down and wade more deliberately. When you find a big rock with one foot and then the other boot finds the other side of the rock when you try to catch your balance, it's time to get out the placards to score your dive.

Except for on very small creeks, a wading staff is an essential piece of equipment for the wading spinner-angler. It acts as both the third leg of a tripod for stability and as a probe to find out what's ahead. It can also let your arm do some of the work when wading through relatively shallow, non-productive water—sort of like ski poles for the skier, except you are just using one arm to give your body a little boost against the current.

When you wade with a staff you will always have two points of contact with the stream bottom. Anchor the staff when you move a foot and make sure your feet are set when you move the staff. When crossing an area with swift current, keep the staff on your upstream side and lean into it. If the staff is below you, the current can easily lift it up off the bottom and cause you to lose your balance. For turbid or deep water the staff can also serve as a searching tool. Having your staff about as long as your waders are tall will let a wet hand indicate that you are getting close to using up all of your freeboard. Using a wading staff in advance of your movement through turbid or unfamiliar water is especially important when moving downstream. If you step into deep water you won't be able to save yourself because the current will be against you.

Attach a cord to the end of your wading staff so that it can float behind you when not in use. Avoid making the attachment a hand grip's distance away from the end. Doing this creates a "notch" or catch point for

Lynda Hayslette wears Korkers and uses a wading staff when fishing Michigan's Grand River.

Leak free, breathable waders helped Mike Haars catch this Alaskan silver.

vines and brush to catch on the tether when you're on the bank walking to the next run.

You can purchase a wading staff or make one from a sturdy broom handle or hardwood sapling. Ski poles without the skirt and hockey stick handles without the blade also work well. Hockey sticks are my favorite and they are free, just visit your local rink to retrieve broken ones before they go to the landfill. If you find another angler fishing your favorite spot you can cross check them out of the way. As long as you don't draw blood you only have to wait two minutes in the penalty box before casting. Okay, just kidding about the cross check, but hockey sticks are very sturdy and won't wobble in strong current when you need them most. And, in addition to facilitating your wading, the staff can also help you get in and out of the river when the bank is steep or slippery.

Wader Repair & Care

If you are, or become, an active wader like myself, you will soon be in the hole- or leak-repair business. This could be the result of a bad encounter with barbed wire, multiflora rose thorns, blackberry vines, or a beaver-sharpened sapling stub. If you have dodged all of these

enemies of waders you will still be fixing a wear spot in the crotch or inseam of your waders.

For a long time now a urethane-based product called Aquaseal has been my permanent solution to any kind of wader damage, including major tears. This material is a very tough and flexible compound. Its special feature is that it also has excellent adhesive qualities.

No patch is needed for tears and holes in your waders. Simply back the damaged area with a removable tape such as masking tape. Take special care to tape the back of the damaged area so that the wader material is in its original position with no puckers. Make sure the area is clean and dry and laying on a flat surface. Liberally apply Aquaseal to the damaged area and spread it with a flat stick. (Note: Popsicle sticks are perfect for this, so wash and save some for future use.) This urethane compound will level itself and spread or run a bit so it's important to keep the repaired area flat during the curing process. The repair will be cured enough for use in eight to twelve hours, but I like to give the repair 24 hours for a complete cure. This is part of the reason why I keep several pairs of waders going all the time. If the damaged area is quite large, a six-inch tear for example, you may want to reinforce the patch by applying the urethane to the other side after removing the tape.

Bill Shake uses a wading staff to cross Oregon's Smith River.

An accelerator called Cotol can be combined with the Aquaseal if a quicker cure is needed. This combination still takes about two hours, so on-stream repair is better left to the ultra-violet-light-activated products. These products harden in minutes when exposed to daylight. They are especially quick when the sun is shining, but they still set up in short order when it's cloudy. The UV-activated adhesives adhere to wet waders, but it's still best to get the area to be patched as dry as possible before applying the material. The UV adhesives work best on neoprene and fabric. They don't adhere well to rubber boots. Even on fabric, the makers of the Aquaseal UV product, which hardens very quickly, recommend letting the adhesive soak in for a minute in a dark (as you can get it) environment before exposing it to the sun for better adhesion. Prior to the recent availability of UV-activated adhesives I used hot-melt patch for a temporary on-stream repair. With any of these quick fixes it's a good idea to make a permanent repair with Aquaseal when you get home. You may have to peel some of the temporary repair material off for best results, but this is not necessary with the Aquaseal UV repair adhesive.

If you're getting damp and clammy because your waders are seeping, usually seams in neoprene waders and seams and pinholes in breathable models, the best way to find the spots is with water. A trouble light lowered into breathable waders in a darkened room may show pinholes, but the sure way is to fill the waders one leg at a time with water and mark the wet spots that form. If you have boot-foot waders where the boots are hard to dry because the insulation is not closed-cell then you will want to perform this operation with the boots inside out. A thin layer of Aquaseal over the small leak spots will keep you dry on your next outing. Spread the sealant out from the hole or seam leak on neoprene waders because sometimes water creeps between the nylon and neoprene. You can also use Aquaseal proactively by coating wear spots before they become leaks.

After a fishing outing it is very important to thoroughly dry your waders. This is especially important for the inside of boot-foot models. If you don't, the fabric may start to rot and weaken the boot, not to mention how bad the mildew will smell. For us old-timers a key piece of equipment for drying boot-foot waders is the archaic bonnet-type hair dryer. The bonnet is discarded and the hose is inserted into the boot for quick drying. If you don't have one I bet a relative does, tucked away back in a closet. You can also reverse a vacuum cleaner to blow warm air into the boot.

A real important fact to remember is that water vapor is lighter than air. If you hang wet boots upside down they will stay wet and likely turn green with mildew inside. For some reason, most modern boot dryers are designed so that you set your boots on them upside down. These dryers just warm the boots with no fan for air movement so they are very inefficient and depend on diffusion of the water-vapor molecules. There are some boot dryers where the warming device is lowered into the upright boot and that makes a lot more sense. From late spring to early fall I let Mother Nature dry my boot-foot breathable waders. I hang them upright in the late-day sun with the boots just resting on the ground. The sun warms up the boots and the water vents out the top.

So, never hang your waders upside down unless they are completely dry. It's best to store boot-foot neoprene waders upright, anyway, with the boots resting on the ground. Obviously you never want to store waders with tight creases, especially neoprene and those with rubber boots. You also want to keep your boots out of the sun and away from ozone-generating electric motors when not in use. Waders are a really important part of a stream angler's tackle and you want to keep them in good shape so they will last.

CHAPTER 6

Fishing Spinners from a Floating Craft

A better title for this chapter might be fishing spinners from and via floating craft. Unlike such techniques such as pulling plugs, backing down divers and bait, and the various side-drifting methods, you will almost never use a boat to fish spinners. Instead the floating craft is used to get you into position to cast and retrieve your lures. A boat allows you to fish rivers that are too big to wade and provides access to smaller rivers in jurisdictions where you are not allowed to wade a stream through private property. Many smaller rivers will also have unwadeable reaches and banks that cannot be traversed.

I confess that I much prefer to fish with my feet firmly planted on the river bottom. This will come as no surprise to regular readers of my articles in *Salmon Trout Steelheader* and other magazines. My rowing skills are mediocre at best, and most of my floating experience has come as a passenger rather than operator of the drift boat or other floating craft. I have never owned a motorized boat or a drift boat. I only made the tiny leap to a personal pontoon craft a few years ago. So, what could I possibly tell you about fishing spinners from a boat? Well, it won't be about running rapids or rowing the boat. It will be about utilizing this mode of transportation to get into position to effectively catch steelhead, trout, and salmon on weighted spinners.

Stealth

We have already stressed the importance of not betraying your presence to trout, salmon, and steelhead you plan to catch with the flashing blade. It might seem that stealth is not necessary in a big river; while these fish probably do feel safer in big water, you'll still greatly enhance your success by not giving fish any clue that something is amiss.

For starters you can make your boat as quiet as possible. Make sure oars and oarlocks don't squeak, or make other sounds, and pad any areas in the boat that are likely to get banged against. As you drift down the river try to anticipate where to anchor the boat in order to most effectively cover the holding water. It's better to anchor prematurely than to float over some fish before getting set up. By getting ready early it's also easier to ease down the anchor and not make a fish-disturbing thud on the bottom. The pulley(s) for your anchor rope should also be silent. When possible, work part way through the run by releasing more anchor rope instead of moving the boat and re-anchoring.

Obviously sweeping tailouts is a great way to catch migrating steelhead and salmon. If the water below the end of the tailout also looks promising, either a deep riffle or quickly dropping into another pool, stay anchored in the tail out and sweep your spinner from above. Again, always be thinking ahead of where fish are likely holding and sneak up on them.

The Bottom Up

When fishing from a boat it's usual to fish each run or section of holding water in a downstream direction. This is obviously the convenient way and it is effective. When pulling plugs or Hotshotting this is probably the best way as you tend to push fish ahead of you until the water gets too shallow. Then, when the fish have no place to go, they will move up and attack the plugs.

Nick Amato uses a personal float boat for mobility on this Oregon coastal stream.

Spinners are also very effective when fished by casting across and down and then swept across the flow. Keep moving downstream and repeating this until the holding water is covered. The distance between arcs depends on water clarity and the confidence you have in the run. But you will do even better when you cover the run working upstream. You will cover the water better as you are less likely to go too fast when moving against the current. And, even more importantly, fishing the run from the bottom greatly increases your chances of catching more than one fish in the run. The reason is that usually the fish will fight downstream from where it's hooked and will not disturb the fish lying above it.

To fish from the bottom up in a boat you need very slack water along the edge of the run to row the boat upstream or you need the water to be wadeable along the edge of the holding water. You must hug the opposite bank and quietly float to the lower end when doing this. It follows that the bottom-up option must be doable based on the configuration of the river and that the run is very likely to hold multiple steelhead or lots of large trout.

Complementary Techniques

Floating a river in a drift boat gives you the option of carrying extra rods for different techniques. At first glance it would seem that fishing spinners would be incompatible with drifting bait, lures, and flies. This would probably be true in a crowded, side-by-side situation. But when you are parked along your own run, drifting and tossing spinners can increase your catch. This is especially true when fishing for salmon and steelhead.

Let's say you are drifting eggs, either bottom-bouncing or under a float, and are having no luck even though the fish are in and the holding water looks great. Fishing the water again with spinners may result in some success. Or maybe the flashing metal also doesn't elicit a strike. Trying the water again with eggs after you have agitated the fish with spinners is often successful. Part of the reason is that you "woke up" the dour fish and part may be that you caused them to shift position slightly so that they more likely to encounter the drifting eggs. When wading I often come to a good pool when someone was drifting eggs and with no success. I ask if I can make a few casts with my spinner

before moving on, and if I get the go-ahead I give the spot a try. Sometimes I will hook a fish and other times I come up empty. But, on a fairly regular basis, as I continue to fish upstream I will look back down and see the drift angler hooked up. Maybe I should have charged a finder's fee for waking up the fish, eh?

When more than one angler is in the drift boat spinners can also be tossed to better cover the water. For example, side-drifters and plug-pullers like fairly clean water for their presentations. There might be some promising but fairly snaggy pocket water adjacent to the runs they are fishing. The spinner-tosser can probe this water with a run-and-gun approach while the oarsman and other anglers are concentrating on their side drifting or Hotshotting.

Float to Wade

As I have already confessed, I would rather wade than fish from a boat. There are many personal watercraft on the market that give you the mobility advantages of floating and let you wade when you fish. You simply wear waders when you row downstream in these mini pontoon craft and pull over to the shallow side of the runs to stand up and cast. Some models have a bar, where you rest your feet when rowing, that goes across the frame so you can stand up and stay corralled in the boat. Others have two foot rests instead of a bar so that it's easy to park/beach and walk out of the boat. If you are going to wade when using this type of boat you will need a tether, but either way these craft are a great way to get you to the fish.

In addition to helping you access water that is not always wadeable or has banks that cannot be walked these craft help you quickly bypass unproductive water. In Michigan, the lower Rifle River is a classic example of a stream where these craft work well. There are wonderful pools but you can have a half mile of flat, "nothing" water between them. I have hiked this stream a lot and it was worth it, but it's nice to have more time to fish by quickly floating through the non-fish-holding water.

Even though I think spinners are better fished via wading there is no doubt that a floating craft gives you access to lots more water and can make covering the water more efficient. And anglers used to floating can give spinners a try when practicing their usual techniques.

CHAPTER 7

Steelhead Biology & Habits;
Best Spinners & Techniques

Most anglers are interested in knowing more about the fish they are trying to catch. The more you know about the habits and life history of your quarry, the more successful you will be. Steelhead have been studied a lot by fisheries scientists and we will try to weave some of that science and knowledge into this chapter to help you catch more of them with weighted spinners.

The Fish

The steelhead is the same species as the rainbow trout. The obvious difference between steelhead and resident rainbow trout is the fact that steelhead migrate to the ocean when they're young and return to the river to spawn as adults. Thus you could also call steelhead anadromous rainbows. In 1992, rainbow trout and other western species of trout were reclassified, they were deemed more closely related to salmon than they were to trout. The scientific name of steelhead was changed from *Salmo gairdneri* to *Oncorhynchus mykiss*. I'm sure the fish taxonomists have good reasons for this change but this angler still thinks these fish are more like trout and keeps the old species name alive as part of his e-mail address.

Rainbow trout that migrate to large lakes, like the Great Lakes, are also frequently called steelhead. Many traditionalist anglers in the Pacific Northwest are of the opinion that the only true steelhead are those rainbows that migrate to salt water and back. As with the reclassification of rainbows, what you call them isn't important when it comes to catching them. But later in this chapter we will try to answer the question of whether lake-run rainbows are steelhead or not, and by doing so will some additional insight to fishing for both.

Early Stream Life

No matter when they enter their natal or stocked stream, most steelhead spawn mid to late winter or spring. In most reasonably fertile streams the young future steelhead or parr spend two years growing to a smolting size of about seven to nine inches. In streams that are lacking in nutrients the river life of these fish will extend to three years and sometimes longer. Many more young steelhead are hatched than make it to smolting size and their battle for survival makes the successful smolts the "cream of the crop". I think that the competition for food and space during their early life contributes to their desire to defend their territory when they return to the river as adult steelhead.

In hatcheries, the time for these fish to reach smolting size is shortened to one year. The constant availability of food and closer-to-ideal water temperatures make this possible. In most cases hatchery yearlings will be ready to smolt when they are stocked or very soon thereafter.

The author with a fresh-run Oregon male steelhead.

As parr begin the smolting process in late spring they turn silvery in color. During this time they are also imprinting to their natal stream so they will know where to return after a period of rapid growth in the ocean or large lake. It's believed that they are imprinted to the reach of river where they resided as well as the whole river. In some systems the smolts must become imprinted to a series of rivers in order to home in on the stream where they were born and raised. In general, the strongest imprint is to the last river before they hit the ocean. For example, virtually all McKenzie River steelhead will find the Columbia but a few will stray and miss the Willamette and a few more may miss the "turn" for the McKenzie.

The imprinting time is relatively short so if hatchery fish are not planted at the right time there could be considerable straying from the planting site. Overall, though, steelhead in both the West and Great Lakes zero in on their natal or planted stream with remarkable regularity.

Ocean & Big Lake

Most steelhead spend one to five years in the ocean or big lake before returning to the tributaries. Some make the trip to spawn more than once, while others save it all up for one trip. Those that return the following fall or winter are called "half-pounders" on the West Coast and "skippers" in the Midwest. They weigh between

Michigan steelhead with a mouthful of silver spinner.

one and three pounds. Some skippers will be sexually immature, but the majority will be precocious males. Some rivers, like Oregon's Rogue, have lots of these fish. In the Great Lakes we seem to have more skippers when river and lake growing conditions are especially good. If smolts left the river at an above-average size and then found plentiful food in the lake, good numbers of them will come back to the river in the fall.

The majority of steelhead make their first trip to the tributary after two or three years in the big water. In general, especially on the West Coast, a high proportion of the hatchery steelhead return as two-salt fish, while the wild fish tend to wait until they have spent three years in the ocean. We don't see as big a difference between hatchery and wild fish in Michigan, probably because all of the hatchery fish have wild parents. Usually the majority of a year class of steelhead will return after three years in the lake, closely followed in numbers by those steelhead that plied the Great Lakes for two years.

Some steelhead will not make their first spawning run until they have fed at sea for four years and, in a few rare cases, five years. These will be your trophy fish as they have concentrated on eating and not procreation. The majority of four-salt fish have already spawned once and aren't much larger than they were on their first spawning run. The reason is that spawning takes a lot out of the fish and it takes some time just to regain the weight lost on their first trip to the river.

Different Mixes

Each river has have its own special mix of returning steelhead and past catch records will help you decide where to go if you are looking for that trophy fish or some smaller hatchery fish for the table. Similarly, the timing of the runs varies in each river system and studying catch records will be an important part of planning your fishing trips.

Obviously a major consideration is whether you are dealing with summer or winter strains of steelhead. There are also runs that occur in fall and spring. The spreading out of the return of steelhead has assured their survival in case of a cataclysmic event that wipes out part of a run. Mother Nature does not put all her eggs in one basket.

Summer steelhead evolved because some spawning habitats were unreachable due to of distance and/ or barriers in the wintertime. For example, with ice and frigid water in northern British Columbia rivers in the winter, if the fish waited until spring there was too much water from spring floods and too little time to travel the considerable distance to the spawning gravel. Strains of summer-run steelhead have also been stocked in streams where there was no reason for summer steelhead to evolve in order to provide a summer river fishery. Indiana's main motivation for stocking Skamania-strain summer steelhead was not to provide a river fishery but was an attempt to keep steelhead in the southern waters of Lake Michigan in summer.

Wild, fall-running steelhead are found in many Great Lakes tributaries with no obvious explanation. There is such a short run to the spawning riffles these fish could easily make the trip in spring. These fish are really great fighters so I'm glad they run even if we don't know why. Rainfall seems to play a big role in how many come up the river in October and November, so Midwest anglers should keep a sharp eye on the weather and hope for periodic heavy downpours. These fish have no urgency to reach the spawning grounds so lower reaches of these rivers are where to intercept these special fish.

Winter weather usually shuts down migration of steelhead in the Great Lakes while this is the time of the main runs on the West Coast. Just like they are in fall for Great Lakes steelhead, freshets are the key to bringing in fish in the Pacific Northwest. If there has been a fairly lengthy dry spell, you definitely want to be on the river after it drops into shape following a good rain. December and January are prime months for hatchery-run steelhead. Wild steelhead also run early in the winter but tend to peak in February and March.

Spring is prime time for the main runs of steelhead in the Midwest. Timing for the peak depends on the severity of winter and how soon spring arrives. Usually late March through April is when most steelhead move into the river. It can be early following a mild winter and will vary by latitude. Runs in most Lake Superior streams won't peak until May. Large impoundments on rivers delay the runs as it takes a while for ice on them to melt and rivers below them to warm. Similarly, the Niagara River, the outlet of Lake Erie, will have a late run if there is a big buildup of ice in Lake Erie.

Spring runs also occur in the West and they are usually lightly fished. At this time of year many anglers are concentrating on spring chinook. Catch records may not help you find these runs because so few anglers are fishing them. But what could be more fun than doing a little detective work and exploring a river with spinners and finding a big pod of spring steelhead?

Migration Rate

Many factors affect the rate at which steelhead move upstream. Water temperature, river height or flow, turbidity of water, distance to spawning riffles, and their degree of sexual maturity all help determine how fast a steelhead moves upstream. If the river is low and cold you are likely to find steelhead in the lower river in deep slow holes near tidewater or the Great Lake. Conversely, if the water temperature is above 40 degrees and it's getting close to spawning time you will do best casting your spinners in the runs in the upper river near the spawning gravel. Learning and recording how steelhead react to weather and water conditions in different rivers at various times will be key to your success. Finding the fish and making a good presentation with your spinner are more important to getting hooked up than choosing the lure with the perfect size and blade finish.

Do They Feed?

Nature has designed steelhead to make the trip to the spawning grounds and back without eating. Even summer steelhead have stored up enough fat to spend more than half a year in the river without taking in a single calorie. While steelhead rarely actively feed, especially winter-run fish, they do remain opportunistic and will take a bait that looks and smells "right" and is presented properly to them. Then, because it tastes and feels good, the steelie will hold on to it long enough for the angler to set the hook. This helps explain why drifting eggs, shrimp, and other food items is so popular among anglers even though steelhead end up expelling

Steelhead will still grab your spinner and jump in 32-degree water.

the bait rather than swallowing it if not hooked. The flash of the spinner may represent the flash of a baitfish that the steelhead fed on in the ocean or Great Lake and trigger a feeding response. More likely though, the steelhead is protecting its space or is just irritated at the shiny intruder when it strikes.

Steelhead or Lake-Run Rainbow

As stated earlier, many anglers believe that the only true steelhead are those anadromous rainbows that travel to the ocean and back. Here we will describe some of the similarities and differences of these migratory rainbows and let you be the judge and learn a bit more about these fish.

While a broad generalization, steelhead that my partners and I have caught in the Pacific Northwest seemed a bit longer and more slender than their lower Great Lakes relatives. They more closely resemble Lake Superior steelhead. This may mean that food is harder to come by in the ocean and Lake Superior than the other Great Lakes. As the food chain in lakes Huron and Michigan is currently being altered by invasive species there is also an apparent slimming down of these fish. Another possibility for the lean shape of western steelhead is that ocean-run fish have to dodge lots of natural predators while nothing eats Great Lakes steelhead after they have reached three or more pounds, except two-legged predators in big boats.

This is further substantiated by the many studies showing better survival of smolts to adults in the lakes compared to the ocean.

On average, river life for young steelhead is also probably easier in the Great Lakes watersheds. In most tributaries to the lower four Great Lakes, young steelhead grow to smolting size in two years. Many of the rivers are fairly rich in nutrients, have very stable flows, and have relatively low gradients with lots of in-stream cover. This results in ideal rearing habitat for young rainbows. Conversely, the majority of steelhead rivers in the Northwest, especially the coastal streams, are lacking in nutrients and have very unstable flow regimes. Very low water in summer and a scarcity of aquatic invertebrates results in rainbow parr needing three or more years to become smolts. The reduced number of salmon, which bring nutrients from the ocean, is also having an impact. Interestingly, the freestone streams flowing into Lake Superior are also typically low in nutrients, have high gradients, and great fluctuations in flow. The result again is the need for three years of growth in the river before smolting.

Another difference between East and West is the return trip for adult steelhead. On average western steelhead must negotiate much faster water with many rapids and falls, and travel much longer distances. So, does this tougher life make them a different fish, a better or tougher fish? And does the easier life make Great Lakes anadromous rainbow trout just a steelhead wannabe?

The ancestors of Michigan's winter steelhead came from California's McCloud River in the 1880s. Wild strains have evolved from these early transplants in many Michigan rivers. The fish have survived for well over 100 years and have endured the sea lamprey invasion and commercial overfishing that resulted in the virtual extinction of lake trout in all the Great Lakes except Lake Superior. Today, Michigan still depends on wild fish in Little Manistee River to supply eggs and milt for all of their hatchery winter steelhead. Has this long period and the many generations of wild steelhead resulted in a current Great Lakes strain that is different from ocean-run fish? Probably. There is no way to tell how these fish might do compared to ocean-run fish unless we plant Little Manistee strain steelhead smolts in a coastal river and see. That is very unlikely to happen.

Do the rigors of life in Pacific Northwest rivers and the ocean result in bigger and stronger steelhead than are found in the Great Lakes? Looking at my catch records, the average sizes between the Great Lakes and

Author with a chunky Lake Erie steelhead.

Washington, Oregon, and Alaska are very similar. As would be expected, Skeena River system steelies average much larger than any others in this group and are not included in the comparison. Despite the average size similarity, I definitely think that your chances for a really big steelhead are better in the Northwest. Fish in the upper teens and low twenties are more common in the West. This is confirmed by my fishing records which show one twenty-pound fish out of a total of about 200 steelhead in Washington and Oregon, while only three 20-plus-pound fish have been landed out of over 8,000 steelies brought to hand in Great Lakes tributaries. While thirty-pounders are very rare but possible in the Northwest, we have yet to reach that size in the Great Lakes. The reason for larger fish in the West may be related to longevity of the fish or to the fact that steelhead in the ocean keep growing in the winter while winter water temperatures in the low to mid 30s cause growth to come to a near standstill for about three months in the Great Lakes.

The question of which fish fights harder usually comes up. The commonly held belief is that ocean-run fish fight harder than Great Lakes steelhead. I think the reason for this arises from the fact that the only experience that most visiting West Coast anglers have had with Great Lakes' fish is in spring when they are spawning or soon will be, and tend to fight poorly.

As an old-timer with many seasons of experience I have come to the conclusion that there is not a lot of difference in fighting ability between ocean- and lake-run fish when compared under similar situations. Nearness to spawning seems to be one of the biggest factors in determining how well these fish battle. Once they have converted a lot of their energy reserves into eggs and milt and are now laden with these sex products, it makes sense that they will not be able to fight as well as they could if they were fresh from the big water and many months away from spawning. Water temperature also plays a role, with the upper forties to upper fifties seeming to bring out the best in steelies. Conversely, very cold temperatures in the low to mid 30s and warm water in the upper 60s can really slow them down. In addition, length of time in the river seems to have an effect. In general, the longer they have been bucking river currents, the less likely they will put up a spectacular battle.

Generally, early-fall-running steelhead in the Great Lakes have given me my best battles. Water temperatures are usually in the low 50s and these fish are six months from spawning. Comparable fish in the West would be fresh-from-the-ocean summer steelhead in streams with similar water temperatures. I have not had the chance to experience these fish but hopefully will get the opportunity.

Keep in mind that the above comparison statements on the steelhead's fighting ability are generalizations. Individual fish may vary a long ways from the average. I've hooked dark steelhead in 33-degree water that put up great resistance with lots of acrobatics and mint-silver fish in 50-degree water that came right in. The exceptions that prove the rule, I guess.

Every steelhead is an individual and there will always be surprises in how they battle the rod. East or West, most anadromous rainbows are good fighters—and often they are spectacular. Whether you believe that lake-run rainbows are steelhead or not, *Oncorhynchus mykiss* is a great fish in the Great lakes and the Pacific Northwest.

Best Spinners & Tactics

All of the advice given earlier for matching spinner selection to the conditions definitely applies to steelhead.

However, in my experience, winter steelhead seem to have a special affinity for spinners with real-silver blades. Perhaps it's just because they reflect more light and are seen by more fish because they can see the spinner from a greater distance. Maybe it's that I have more confidence in silver. I do know that when the sun comes out or the water clears, I usually change to a smaller silver spinner rather than switching to gold or copper when fishing for winter steelhead.

Summer steelhead are a different story. These fish, especially the Skamania strain, seem to like orange a lot, so I will often use a fluorescent-orange-bladed spinner when fishing for these fish. When I want some flash I switch to a copper blade because of the reddish-orange cast to its flash as opposed to gold or silver. I really like to have fluorescent orange as part of my spinners throughout the year so virtually all of my steelhead spinners have fluorescent orange tape on the back of the blade. Putting tape on the back of the blade may seem odd but it allows you to get full benefit of the flash from the front of the blade while showing bright color when the steelhead approaches from behind the spinner. The color will also show to a lesser degree as the spinner sweeps by the fish. The spinner will actually change its appearance as the angle to the fish changes. I have been putting tape on the back of all my spinner blades for about 40 years now and it seems to be helping. But since I don't fish unadorned spinners I will never know for sure. Probably, just like silver blades for winter steelhead and orange for summer-runs, I have confidence in the tape and that alone helps me catch more fish.

Covering water and maximizing hang time are especially important tactics when fishing for steelhead. While in some rivers and some situations steelhead can keg up in a small area, most of the time they will be spread out. And, as we have already described, spinners attract strikes from a considerable distance and you will make them more effective by covering lots of water. Invading the steelhead's space by hanging the spinner in the current is also really important. So whenever possible get above the fish and sweep the spinner across the holding water. Try to keep the spinner moving laterally as slowly as possible to maximize the time it's in the steelhead's view. Don't hesitate to give line and back it down through a good area when spinner has swung around and you are directly above it. This keeps the spinner in the strike zone when the current would cause it to rise if it was just hanging it in place.

CHAPTER 8

Salmon Biology & Habits
Best Spinners & Techniques

There are five species of Pacific salmon that frequent the waters of North America. Atlantic salmon more closely resemble trout and we will cover them in the next chapter. All five species of Pacific salmon strike spinners and can be caught on their spawning runs. Chinook or king salmon and coho or silver salmon are the primary sport species and the most widely distributed. Dog or chum, red or sockeye, and pink or hump-backed can also provide fine sport even though their range is not as great and they are not as popular. We will describe all five and talk about adapting your spinner-fishing techniques to their habits.

Chinook Salmon

The king or chinook salmon is, as the name might imply, the largest member of the salmon family. The sport-caught record is over 90 pounds, and specimens well over 100 pounds have been captured commercially. It stands to reason that these fish would have the longest life cycle in order to reach their large size. Like all of these salmon in the lower 48, chinook spawn in the fall and typically young chinook smolt late in the following spring. This allows them to successfully spawn in rivers that would be too warm in the summer for salmon and trout to survive. In northern Canada and Alaska spawning time is backed up into the summer to give the chinook more time to grow to smolting size by late the following spring. Adults may start their spawning migration in spring, summer, or fall. Some very precocious male chinook return to the river after just one summer in the lake or ocean. They will be sexually mature even though they are barely a foot long. My "reverse record" was an eight-incher caught in Michigan's Grand River. I'm guessing he didn't fare too well trying to spawn with the twenty-pounders. While these very small jacks are the exception there will be fair numbers of two- and three-year-old jacks and some three-year-old females will return to spawn. Most adult spawning chinook will be four years old and the big guys will have spent five and six or more years at sea.

As everybody knows, chinook and other Pacific salmon die after spawning. Their carcasses are broken down by bacteria and eaten by invertebrates that in turn provide sustenance for the next generation of salmon. When adult salmon enter the rivers they lose their ability to swallow and digest food. Ironically, a big gob of eggs is still a great bait for these fish on their river migration even though they cannot eat. It's probably a memory thing, and it smells and tastes good to these fish. When salmon were introduced into the Great Lakes in the late 1960s the plan was for them to just provide a lake fishery and control the exploding alewife population. Anglers were accurately told that the salmon would not eat in the river but were not told they could still be caught in rivers and given advice on catching them. So, many decided that snagging was the only way to "catch" these fish and it took a long time to eradicate legal snagging. Some still want instant gratification and illegally try to snag salmon. I really have trouble with those that degrade these wonderful fish into pieces of meat to be dragged from the river.

Today, most Great Lakes anglers have learned how to catch these salmon on their spawning run.

The fishing has also been helped by the fact that Great Lakes strains of chinook have evolved. Because fisheries biologists were mostly interested in creating a lake fishery they brought in the toolie strain of chinook. These fish darken up even before they hit tidewater and are deemed a poor river fish. Over time chinook have begun their river migration in Michigan earlier and earlier and are coming upstream as bright-silver fish. These new "Michigan strain" chinook are more aggressive and still provide good table fare when caught in the river well prior to spawning.

Fishing weighted spinners is a very good approach to catching river kings in the Pacific Northwest and Great Lakes area. Fresh-run chinook are the most eager biters but it's amazing how these fish will continue to attack an intruding lure until they are close to death. Large-bladed spinners that turn slowly are especially good for chinook. The "thump" of a slowly turning size 5 or larger spinner definitely gets their attention.

Chinook tend to be light shy. This is true in the ocean and Great Lakes and even more so when they enter the river. On bright sunny days the bite is often over as soon as the first rays hit the river surface. Most of the time, cloudy, rainy days give you the best chance to aggravate king salmon into grabbing your spinner. I wrote 'most of the time' because if the day is really dark salmon will often be focusing on moving upstream. When they decide to head up river it's harder to get them to strike than it is in the sunshine. So, usually it's the middle part of a cloudy day when chinook are apt to rest and bite best.

While these salmon do like big spinners they don't necessarily want a bright spinner. Brass, copper, and nickel, which reflect less light, are often a better choice than real silver. Some anglers go to black blades but I have not had much luck with them and have had problems with accidentally snagging salmon because they don't see the spinner in time to either hit it or get out of the way. While just a tendency, chinook seem to have a preference for green tape on the back of the blade. This is similar to steelhead liking orange. It's not a sure thing but I almost always try green first for chinook. I also will use two shades of green for contrast. Usually I couple fluorescent yellow or chartreuse with fluorescent lime or dark green. If the day is bright and the water is clear, using just dark green can be the best plan.

Coho Salmon

Silver or coho salmon are very popular river fish. It helps that they often seek out smaller rivers that are easily reached by anglers on foot. These salmon have a shorter life cycle than chinook and thus don't grow as large. Typically they have a three-year life cycle and spend half of that time in the river. Hatchery coho also have to spend half their life in the hatchery since they can't be raised to smolting size in just one winter. In Alaska, adult silver salmon run in late summer and early fall, while most in the lower 48 migrate up river in fall. They overlap the fall chinook run but almost always peak later. Some wild strains in the Pacific Northwest run in the winter. These fish are larger fish on average, probably because they fed in the ocean for a few extra months.

Since young coho spend a year and a half in the river these fish can only successfully spawn in rivers that support trout or other coldwater fish all year. Often these fish spawn in small tributaries of the river they are running. Keep this in mind as you fish for them. If you come across a creek flowing into the river, fish the closest pool or holding water to the creek mouth really hard. In the Great Lakes a fair number of coho salmon return as jacks. These fish weigh about two pounds after one summer in the lake. They grow much faster during the second year in the lake as they have gotten big enough to feed on alewives and other forage fish. A small number of silver salmon stay in the ocean or lake an extra year and these will be the trophy fish pushing 20 pounds.

Since their growing time is basically crunched into one spring and summer in the Great Lakes, their size at maturity is a really good indication of lake conditions. When they were first stocked in 1966 there was an abundance of alewives and these fish averaged twelve to fifteen pounds when they headed to the rivers in fall of 1967. In 1976, one of the coho salmon that ate alewives for an extra year in Lake Michigan became the state record and the near world record at 30.5 pounds. Around the same time a 39-pound coho arrived at the egg-taking weir on the Little Manistee River. Instead of releasing this fish upstream it was killed and mounted. I definitely think it would have been a much better plan to release it and see if this world record might be caught by a steelhead angler. I'm guessing that if replica mounts had progressed then to the point they are now, the fish could have

A male coho in full spawning colors.

been released and a mount still made for the DNR to show off.

Silver salmon seem to be, on average, more aggressive and better biters on their river migration than other Pacific salmon. Perhaps this is because of their longer time in the river as young salmon battling for space and food. While often not as strong and persevering as other salmon on the end of your line these fish will spend the most time on the surface. On a number of occasions I have been fooled into thinking I had hooked into a steelhead only to discover a bright coho lying in my net at the end of the struggle. The takes of silver salmon can range from savage strikes to some of the softest you will ever encounter. On many occasions I have tried to lift my spinner from the water at the end of a retrieve only to discover that a coho was attached. As usual, sweep casts are a good presentation for these fish, and you will frequently find them in relatively slow current. Thus, it's important that your spinner spins at very slow retrieves and will keep revolving when hung in weak currents. Silver-plated blades are usually the best choice and red, orange, and pink are good colors for blade tape, beads, and tubing on the hook.

Pink Salmon

Pink or humpback salmon are the most plentiful of all salmon and also the smallest. They tend to get little respect from many anglers because they are so common, small, and their flesh deteriorates rapidly after they enter the stream. However, on ultralight spinning tackle and small spinners they can provide great sport.

Pink salmon normally only live two years and this is why they rarely get large. We got excited in Michigan a few years ago when we started catching what seemed to be world-record pink salmon. That bubble was burst when it was determined that the big pinks were really chinook-pink salmon hybrids. These fish were given the name "pinooks".

Pink salmon usually spawn in early fall in the Pacific Northwest and Great Lakes. They head back to the ocean soon after the young absorb the yolk sac so their river life is short with most of it spent in the gravel incubating and hatching. In the West they have a fairly rigid two-year life cycle so that most streams only receive a run every two years. If a river does get a run

Mike Haars with a male pink salmon.

every year usually the odd or even year is much stronger than the other. On their spawning run the male develops a large hump on its back, hence their other common name.

In the ocean pink salmon feed almost exclusively on plankton and thus are rarely caught by sports anglers plying the open sea. Once they enter rivers they will strike lures as they protect their space. Using the ultra-light spinning tackle that you would use when trout fishing can result in lots of fish landed when the run is on. Most of these salmon are the size of large trout, two to four pounds, so size one and two spinners are just right. Part of the bad rap they sometimes get is that they are hooked on heavy tackle meant for other salmon and thus don't appear to fight hard. Pound for pound, that is not the case.

The initial lack of respect for these fish is really illustrated in how they came to be in the Great Lakes. In 1955 Ontario fisheries personnel were going to try stocking pink salmon in Lake Superior but changed their mind about introducing these fish. They flushed the fingerlings down a drain which turned out to be connected to the lake and "stocked" them anyway. Some returning adults strayed into various nearby tributaries and, with time, the pinks expanded throughout the upper Great Lakes.

The humpback's two-year cycle and short stream stay helped them adapt and spread through the upper lakes. Unlike most of the populations on the West Coast, these salmon haven't stuck with the two-year life cycle in the Great Lakes. The reason is the relatively low levels of plankton in Lake Superior probably required the some of the salmon to spend three seasons in the lake to reach maturity. Thus there are runs every year in Great Lakes tributaries but the heaviest runs tend to still be in the odd numbered years. Again due to the paucity of plankton, Great Lakes' pink salmon have adapted and added small fish to their diet. This change in their feeding habits explains why they became part of the troller's catch and how they might reach record size until it was learned that the big pinks were hybrids.

Sockeye Salmon

Sockeye or red salmon are the most sought after salmon for the table. They have the reddest flesh of any salmon, hence their name. These salmon require a lake with spawning gravel above it in their home rivers. These fish spawn in the river above the lake or other tributaries to the lake. After the young salmon hatch and absorb their yolk they move down into the lake to grow to smolting size. This can take one or two years depending on the food availability of the lake.

In the ocean these fish feed strictly on plankton. This regimen is likely the reason for their deep red flesh as they filter feed on the zoo plankton in the water column. Most spend two years in the ocean and return as six-to-ten pound fish with a small percentage reaching higher weights. When these fish first enter the river they are highly sought after by anglers that love their fine flavor. However, probably because of their feeding habits as adults they can be difficult but not impossible to entice into striking. Spinners and other lures will often be ignored. Because of this strong reluctance to hit lures and baits many employ lining techniques to catch these fish. With this technique a fly or other small lure or bait is drifted on a long leader through schools of fish. The line catches in their mouth and passes through until the hook arrives. For me this technique doesn't work because I believe that, in sport fishing, the fish must make the final decision to strike a lure or inhale a bait. However, this technique is condoned by a large contingent of anglers as long as the fish end up hooked in the mouth. The great battle and fine flavor of the sockeye probably influence the fact that the majority think it is okay to passively snag these fish.

As these fish move up stream and get closer to spawning, spinners will take lots of fish. The salmon seem to become more and more territorial when the time for redd making gets close. As with other salmonids, a real key is to hang your spinner in their face as long as possible to invoke a positive response. Sockeye salmon put up a spirited battle at whatever stage of their river migration that you hook them but are especially strong fighters when they have newly arrived in the river.

Chum Salmon

Chum salmon are on the opposite end of the epicurean chart from sockeye salmon. Their other common name is definitely not derived from the way they fight. Instead these dog salmon, especially the males, develop large teeth on their spawning run that resemble canine teeth on a dog.

Like pink salmon, the river life of the young chum salmon is very short. These fish spawn in the lower reaches of coastal rivers and when baby salmon or fry hatch and emerge from the gravel they quickly head downstream. They stay and grow in the estuary until they are ready to tackle the ocean.

Chum salmon readily hit spinners on their river migration. They are the second largest Pacific salmon, averaging slightly larger than coho salmon. They will put up a spirited battle with a never-give-up attitude. Many anglers think that chum salmon are stronger than king salmon of the same size. Use the same sizes and finishes that you would for coho salmon.

Pacific salmon often enter their natal or stocked rivers in large schools. They are almost always more numerous than steelhead. As you fish a river it is typical to find holes filled with lots of fish as the school hangs together to a fair extent on its river migration. These fish are very aware of each other as they jockey for a resting spot of their liking. My experience has been that it can be very difficult eliciting a strike with a spinner when big numbers of salmon are present in a pool. My success greatly improves when I try to pick off resting fish in small, shallower runs and pockets between the pools full of salmon milling about. Perhaps it's because the solitary fish or small group have found a spot to their liking and want to protect it by blasting your spinner. Or maybe it's just that they can concentrate on your spinner without worrying about and being jostled by a bunch of other salmon. Don't be afraid to leave the loaded pool. Use your river-reading skills and move along until your spinner flashes by a cooperative salmon.

CHAPTER 9

Trout Biology & Habits; Best Spinners & Techniques

We can divide trout into three groups. The western trout, which were reclassified as salmon, include the rainbow and cutthroat trout. The remaining true trout are the brown trout and Atlantic salmon. Chars are the final group and include brook, dolly varden, and lake trout. Most all of these species of trout have migratory or anadromous strains. While we will cover these wanderers, we are going to concentrate on stream resident trout in this chapter.

Rainbow Trout

Rainbow trout are native to the west side of the Rocky Mountains but they have been very widely introduced all over the world. They are easily the most popular trout. You can also say they are the most modified trout with a large number of strains having been developed by man. Nature has also added to the variety of rainbows with its diverse habitats. These fish range from the "leopard rainbows" in Alaska that must do all their growing only in the summer months, yet still reach huge sizes, to red-band strains in the high desert that at times must endure water temperatures in the 80-degree range.

Except for a few artificially modified strains, rainbow trout are spring spawning fish. This sets them and cutthroat trout apart from the true trout and the chars. This trait helps them be successful in some streams in cold climates. There will be times when anchor ice develops in streams in the winter. This is not a problem for very mobile fingerling rainbows that hatched the previous spring but can be the end of the line for the developing eggs and sac fry of fall spawning species. The anchor ice can prevent oxygenated water from flowing through the gravel and result in the suffocation of the developing trout.

Spring spawning also results in trout that are very hungry following their procreation chores. So when the water conditions allow you can expect very good fishing for rainbows in the late spring and early summer. These fish are aggressive feeders much of the time and especially so after spawning.

Rainbows have a strong liking for fast-water habitats. Often they are called riffle trout. They are also trout of relatively open water. Stream resident rainbows are still cover oriented but they seem to be more willing to "expose" themselves than other species. While they will feed at night rainbows seems to prefer the daylight hours for filling their stomachs. That is good news for spinner-tosser. There are approximately equal numbers of rainbows and browns in one of my favorite Montana streams. When the sun is high the rainbows keep hitting while it becomes much harder to draw the browns out from the cover.

Size one and two spinners from 1/8 to 1/6 ounces in shiny metallic finishes work well for rainbow trout. Silver and gold work well and sometimes copper is the most productive. Small streams often require upstream casts but, just like for steelhead, when you can sneak

Montana cutthroat caught on a minnow plug.

above the holding water and sweep across you will really get the rainbow's attention. While spinners with French type blades are best for all-around use, the Panther Martin style in-line bladed spinners are great for sweeping deep riffles and runs.

As always, moving right along is the plan when fishing for resident rainbows. While they are less shy you still will do best if you avoid letting them know of your presence. Rainbows are hard fighters and leap often so you will want to get hooked up to them often.

Cutthroat Trout

Like rainbows, cutthroat trout are also native to the Rocky Mountains but were found mostly on the east side of the Rockies. There are many strains or subspecies of cutthroat that evolved in isolated drainages with some even reaching the status of a separate species. Cutthroats have been propagated in hatcheries and introduced to other waters but not anywhere near to the extent that rainbows have. There are a number of instances where rainbows were introduced into native cutthroat waters and this usually had a negative effect on the cutthroat population. Cutthroat trout also spawn in the spring and rainbows may interbreed with them resulting in hybrid offspring called cuttbows.

Cutthroat trout feed aggressively and are often considered easier to catch than rainbows. Thus when the two species exist in the same stream this is one of the possible reasons that leads to the belief that rainbows will out compete and displace cutthroats. As far as coexisting, their preferred habitats minimize competition. While the rainbows are hanging out in the riffles and quick runs the cutthroat will be more numerous in the deeper, slower water. There will be exceptions but you can almost predict which species you will catch in streams harboring both by where you've cast and retrieved your spinner. The same French type spinners we described for hooking rainbows will work for cutthroat trout. Just concentrate on the slower, deeper water when targeting cutts.

Some cutthroat trout also spend time at sea. These fish are called coastal cutthroat or harvest trout. They are not your typical anadromous fish that goes out to the ocean and feeds for several years before returning to spawn. Instead these fish usually stay fairly close to the river mouth and may even go back and forth on a regular basis. The usual plan is for them to spend the late spring and summer in the estuary or near-shore ocean and then head back to the river in late summer or fall, hence the name harvest trout. They spawn in late winter or early spring and repeat the process.

Most of my encounters with sea-run cutthroat have come when fishing for winter steelhead. They are not bashful about striking a size four or five steelhead spinner but you will probably do better with smaller spinners if you want to target these fish. They are great fun and provide action when steelhead are scarce. A size three spinner would be a good compromise, large enough to attract a steelhead take but not too big for the typically one-to three-pound cutthroats.

Brown Trout

Brown trout are not native to North America however, for the most part, they have been a welcome addition. But, just like when the rainbow displaces native cutthroat, many get upset when the brown (or rainbow) out-competes the native brook trout in the eastern United States. Brown trout came from Europe and have been with us since the 1880s. These fish enjoy a special following thanks to their propensity to take flies on the surface.

Brown trout have been my main quarry when fishing southern Michigan creeks with spinners for trout. I have developed great respect for their smarts or wariness. They are extremely cover oriented and have the reputation of being difficult to catch, especially the large specimens. There is always great satisfaction when a big brown is lured from its lair and convinced to engulf your spinner. One of the big advantages of spinners is that they represent a substantial meal and give the brown trout reason to leave the confines of the undercut bank or large log.

While these fish do inhabit the deep, slow holes in streams, they will move to shallow faster water to feed. So, as mentioned earlier in the techniques chapter, you want to run your spinner by likely feeding stations. The brown trout will be much more interested in your spinner when they are actively feeding. Brass spinners in size one are my go-to lures for brown trout. While spinners don't resemble any natural food, the gold flash may match the coloration of the crayfish and sculpins that browns favor.

Anadromous browns are called sea trout and are principally found in Europe. They have, along with rainbows, been very successfully introduced into South American trout rivers. Brown trout are stocked in the Great Lakes to provide near-shore fisheries. These fish spawn in the fall and, while most spawn in lakes, some do run the tributaries. Typically they move upstream in October and spawn in early November. After spawning most browns remain in the rivers until early spring. While you can target these fish, especially in some Lake Ontario tributaries, they are usually a bonus catch when steelhead fishing. They strike spinners especially well after they are done spawning. The same spinners that work for steelhead will catch lake-run browns, although polished brass and gold spinners are favored by the browns. Fluorescent red is a good color for the tubing and tape on the back of the blade for these wandering brown trout.

Brown trout and author's spinner box.

Atlantic salmon are closely related to brown trout and are of the same genus, *Salmo*. Most fisheries for Atlantics are "flies only" so we will only touch on them briefly in this book. There are some ocean-run Atlantics that are not restricted to fly-fishing and many landlocked populations exist where you can fish for them with spinners. These fish are similar to summer steelhead in that they run rivers in the summer. However, like brown trout, they spawn in the fall. Spinners and spinner techniques for these salmon are very similar to the ones you would use for steelhead. Often the streams are low and, at times, warm so extra stealth is needed and if your stream thermometer reads in the upper 60s or higher you should seek other quarry.

Brook Trout

Brook trout are native to the eastern half of North America but they too have been transplanted. Just like rainbows have caused problems with native brookies in the east, brook trout have become nuisances in parts of the west. Brook trout are really char and tend to grow more slowly and not live as long as browns and rainbows. Thus they are smaller on average than other stream trout. Like all members of the char family, brook trout spawn in the fall.

With the cutting of the forests in the east and the introduction of browns and rainbows, the stronghold of brook trout has become the headwater streams. There are exceptions but most of the good brookie fishing is found in creeks and small streams. When available, slower streams tend to favor brook trout too. They can spawn on much smaller sized gravel than browns. Many think that brookies favor and need much colder water than brown trout. That turns out to be not the case. Some of the best brook trout streams in my home state of Michigan are on the warm side and the brookies must compete with creek chubs.

Size zero and one spinners work well when chasing brookies in the creeks. Just like the browns they like to take advantage of a substantial meal. Brightly colored silver and gold spinners will get attacked by these diminutive char when they are hungry. Brookies are considered dumb because they are often aggressive and intolerant of the angler's intrusion. Large brook trout are not dumb or they wouldn't have survived to be measured in pounds instead of inches. While brook trout can live in water as warm as brown trout can, they

Brookie caught on a small brass spinner.

are more active at temperatures below 50 degrees than browns and rainbows so a brook trout stream can be a good choice early in the spring.

Coaster brook trout are very similar to coastal cutthroat in that they are not truly anadromous. These fish exist in a few streams on the east coast and the upper Great Lakes. There used to be strong populations of these fish but their numbers dwindled. They are currently making a comeback in the Great Lakes with the help of several angling groups. These fish grow larger than the year-around stream inhabitants. They move into the tributaries to spawn in fall and follow the smelt in spring to feed. Small silver spinners work well and in spring brookies will spice up the steelhead fishing.

Lake trout are closely related to brook trout but for the most part are not considered a stream fish. In northern Canada these fish reside in the riverine sections of river systems that flow from lake to lake. In the Great Lakes most of the lake trout spawn on reefs in the lake but some, for unknown reasons, migrate up rivers to spawn. The peak time for this spawning migration is late October through November. Like coasters, lake trout also move into Great Lakes tributaries in the spring to feed on spawning smelt. Silver spinners with green bodies and tape seem to be especially attractive to lake trout. Splake are hybrids of lake and brook trout and while they rarely are present in rivers they do offer good sport on spinners in the shallows of the lakes in which they are stocked.

Terri Bedford with a lake trout at the 6th Street Dam on MI's Grand River.

Dolly Varden Trout

Dolly Varden are the most common char of western North America. They are present in many stream systems in the lower 48 but become more numerous as you move north. There are both anadromous and stream-resident populations. These fish spawn in the fall and grow slowly in rivers. It may take the young of anadromous strains four years before they head to sea.

Most of my experience with Dollies has come when fishing for steelhead in British Columbia and Alaska. These fish enthusiastically chase your spinner and really keep you busy between steelhead encounters. At one time they were considered trash fish that ate salmon eggs and smolts. This is not the case today as many anglers treasure these beautiful fish and the fast fishing action they provide. Anglers also have come to realize that rainbows exhibit the same feeding habits so why "pick on" Dollies. Dollies like slower water than the rainbows they often share the river with and tend to fight their battle under water. They often play second fiddle when showy rainbows are present but definitely add variety to your catch.

Dolly Varden trout are very closely related to bull trout and were long considered the same species. This changed in the late 1970s, but, as you might expect, these char are difficult to tell apart. Usually it will be one or the other in a watershed and bull trout tend to live in cold inland streams and are seldom anadromous. In most watersheds they are a protected species but there are still catch-and-release opportunities.

Arctic char are also closely related to Dolly Varden trout. These fish live in the far north with many of them anadromous. In Alaska you frequently hear the half-joking remark that if you can drive to the river the fish are Dolly Varden but if you have to hire a guide or fly in they are arctic char. I do think that arctic char are easier to distinguish from Dolly Varden char than bull trout. Using the same approach you would when fishing for steelhead is a good way to catch anadromous arctic char. These fish hit the same spinners and fight a very tenacious underwater battle. When I fished for arctic char, brook and lake trout in the same river, the only difference in the fight was in the size of the fish. The arctic char did seem to prefer somewhat faster water than the lakers and brookies though.

Resident-Trout Tactics

While we have described many of the trout forms that are anadromous or migratory in this chapter we are going to concentrate on resident trout as we summarize thoughts and give additional tips on tactics and spinners. Resident is a key word. When we fish a trout stream we are fishing for trout that live there all the time. These fish are very aware of their surroundings. They know where the best cover is located, where the best feeding stations lie, and the escape routes to safety. Resident trout are very aware of what is normal and anything that is not alarms them and makes them difficult to catch. I know I keep repeating myself, but stream stealth is especially important when fishing for wild resident trout.

Fishing in an upstream direction is always the best plan when fishing for resident trout. Most of the time you will want your spinner to land well upstream of the trout's suspected lair in order to keep from spooking it. There will be times, however, when a seductive plop will lure a trout out of deep cover. Trout feed a lot on terrestrial insects so dropping that spinner close to the bank will pay off. There have been times when I was sure the trout saw the spinner in the air as they "caught" it as soon as it hit the water.

Lots of times trout, especially browns, will follow behind a spinner and then just inhale it. So stay on your toes and be ready to set the hook when you detect

The author with an arctic char from northern Quebec.

during the retrieve. Many strikes will occur right at this point. The turn is obviously easily accomplished when you cast down and across, but you can still do it on a straight upstream cast. Just extend your rod straight upstream near the end of the retrieve and stop reeling, allowing the spinner to swing around in the current under your rod. This turn also works on anadromous fish and is especially effective when you have lure tape on the back of your blade.

Finally, spinners seem to work especially well in streams where crayfish are part of the trout's diet. A number of years ago I was flipping my spinner to the top of a deep run and my cast came up short. I noted there was a loop on the spool and since the spinner was already on the bottom I decided to pull the loop off before retrieving the spinner. Just as I picked the spinner up off the bottom a nice brown nailed it. This scenario repeated itself a few weeks later and the proverbial lightbulb lit-up in my head. I now allow my spinner to sink to the bottom in likely lairs on a regular basis. Of course you must pick spots where the substrate is likely free of wood, rocks, or plant life that would hang up your lure. I always make a couple of conventional cast and retrieves first before letting the spinner sink to the bottom. This presentation works best on sandy substrates because, I think, the spinner kicks up a puff of sand when you start the retrieve. I also think the fluttering of the spinner as it sinks to the bottom gets the trout's attention as they are usually right on it when you pick it up. Adding the "crayfish cast" to your repertoire will put more trout on the end of your line.

a slight change in the resistance of the spinning lure. Often it will be just a leaf or blade of grass that hung on the hook but you sure don't want to discover that it was a nice trout just as it expels your spinner.

Watching your spinner track through the water is a good plan whenever possible and is especially helpful when fishing for stream-resident trout. If you see the trout just suck in your lure you can set the hook even when you have felt nothing. Watching the spinner track through the water will also help you guide it close to cover. Sometimes you can also see how the trout react to it when they show interest but don't hit. If you are getting follows but no strikes you may want to change to a different spinner. If the spinner seems to be spooking the trout, changing to a smaller or duller lure may be just the ticket. If a trout is just steadily following, speeding up the lure is more likely to draw a strike than slowing it down. This gives the illusion that the spinner is alive and has seen the trout and is now trying to escape.

Another trick that will increase your success with spinners is what I call the "magic turn". No matter which way you cast in relation to the current, try to make the spinner change direction at some point

A brown trout that got hungry in the middle of a Michigan winter.

CHAPTER 10

Making Your Own Spinners

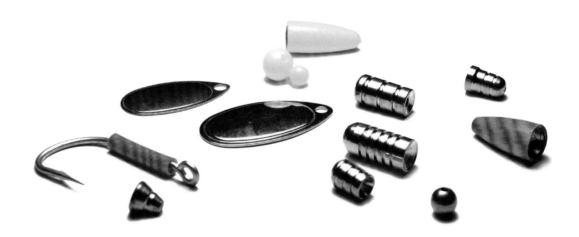

Weighted spinners have been a very popular lure for a long time. There are many commercial spinners on the market that will do a great job of getting you hooked up to trout and salmon. Mepps, Super Vibrax, and Panther Martin are brands that immediately come to mind. Warren's Double Loon is a lesser known spinner but was principally developed for trout and salmon. It's the only current commercial spinner I know of that puts lure tape on the back of the blade. This is a very important concept and one that I have been applying to my spinners for about 40 years.

So, if there are good-quality spinners out there that are ready to fish, why build your own? The main answer is to save money, but you can also build a better spinner. By better I mean one that works better and designed for the water you fish and the species you fish for. Making your own spinners is also a very pleasurable activity and a great way to spend your leisure time while waiting for the rivers to come back in shape or thaw out.

Building spinners is easy. You simply assemble component parts with no carving, painting or other skill-requiring artistic endeavors. The main components of a weighted spinner are the blade, body, shaft, and hook. We will describe each component group in detail, provide recipes on putting some together, assemble various types and sizes, and make the top loop. At the end we will give tips on saving your spinners from the river bottom.

Blades

There are a huge number of spinner blade styles and finishes on the market today. We are going to simplify things and focus on the best blades for river fishing.

The standard French or domed blade is the preferred blade for most river fishing because it spins at slower retrieve speeds than most other blades. We will also build spinners with Panther Martin or in-line style blades. Weighted spinners are often described as in-line spinners to differentiate them from the spinner bait or safety-pin style jig and spinner combination used by bass anglers. This is confusing because the highly curved blades with the hole in the center are described as in-line blades as opposed to most blades that have a hole at their top and are combined with a clevis when made into a spinner. So we will use "weighted spinner" to describe any spinner blade that is combined with a weighted body and reserve the term "in-line" for those spinners made with that special blade.

Spinner blades are available in a variety of finishes. Polished brass, copper, nickel, black nickel, silver, and gold are common metallic finishes. You can also buy painted blades and unpolished brass if you want to paint your own. Polished brass, copper, and silver blades can be lacquered to prevent tarnishing. that are. Hammered blades are available but you will want to choose smooth blades if you plan on using lure tape.

Home-built spinner fools a nice brown.

Real silver-plated blades can be purchased in a shiny or matte finish. As we have already discussed in an earlier chapter, silver reflects more light than the other metals. However, shiny silver plate also acts as a mirror and will reflect the surroundings. So in a dark stream situation the shiny silver blade will not be as visible as a matte or frosty silver blade. I strongly recommend purchasing matte silver blades. Then if you want to make some of them shiny you can quickly and easily polish them with a baking soda and water paste. You can also renew tarnished silver blades this way. It is important not to use strong metal polishes on silver-plated blades. If you do, your silver blade will soon turn to polished brass as the silver is quickly removed.

Copper and brass tarnish easily and much more quickly than silver. For steelhead and salmon I like my blades to be shiny so even though brass and copper are easy to polish, I purchase some lacquered copper and real-gold blades for larger spinners. By doing this I know that I won't have to rue failing to polish blades between trips when I open my spinner box for a brass or copper spinner. For size-one trout spinners I stick with plain copper and polished brass with no lacquer. I then purposely let some of the blades on my spinners become tarnished. The muted flash of these spinners is just right for browns and rainbows when the sun is out and the stream is very clear.

Choosing the proper blade thickness is important when building spinners. Most blades are stamped out of brass sheets .018, .025, or .032 inches thick. Much has been written about the advantage of the extra-thick, .032-inch blades. The heavier blade will spin slower and this was touted as being more attractive to steelhead and salmon. Well, a slow spin is a good thing but no spin is awful. There are ideal thicknesses for each blade size and good reasons for choosing them.

Size 0, 1, & 2 spinner blades are best made out of .018-inch brass. These blades need to spin right away and at slow speeds. Frequently you are retrieving them downstream with the current. Most commercial small spinners are made with .025-inch brass and you have to pull hard to get them started. When you are fishing small streams or pocket water you need the blade to start turning as soon as the spinner hits the water and you start the retrieve.

The best all-around thickness for size 3, 4 & 5 blades is .025 inches. Basically we are matching and balancing blade thickness with surface area. Using .032-inch brass for these blades will slow them down when sweeping fast

water and of course there is no problem keeping them spinning against the fast current. But when the spinner sweeps into the soft water ahead of a boulder, where the steelhead is likely to be laying, the heavy blade stops spinning and you are out of luck. Or, you have to pull it away from the fish to keep it spinning. Size 6 is a transition size and both .025- and .032-inch-thick blades will work. Brass of the .032-inch thickness works well for the huge size 7 and 8 blades that some king salmon anglers favor. Personally, I seldom use spinners larger than size 5 for anadromous fish and most of the time I've got a size 3 or 4 tied on to my line. Another option for fast water is the in-line style blade. These blades have less water resistance and stay down better than French blades. They are also noisier and send out more vibrations than French blades so they can be a good alternative to using a very large French blade when the water is up and visibility is low.

Clevises are required with French blades and are an important component of a well-designed spinner. Most commercial spinners have folded clevises because they are stronger. Stirrup type or "Easy-Spin" clevises spin much better because there is less metal contacting the shaft and therefore less friction. On occasion these clevises can be crushed or pinched, usually by a big fish. This would ruin the spinner for the casual angler and thus most spinner manufacturers use the folded clevises. But if this happened to you, you could probably bend the clevis back to its original shape or simply re-make the spinner on a new shaft with a new clevis.

Shafts

All weighted spinners are built on a wire shaft. You can work from a coil of tempered straight spring wire or pre-cut shafts. The shafts can be just a straight piece of wire, one with a closed loop on one end, or with an open loop on one end. The wire should be stainless steel. The wire diameter varies with the spinner size. In general, .024-inch wire works well for size 0 spinners and .026 is a good choice for size 1 and 2 spinners. You should move up to .031-inch wire for size 3 and larger spinners. Using wire with a diameter of .035 inches is an option for very large spinners.

Starting with open-wire shafts is usually the best plan when building spinners. They give you the most options relative to shaft length and also allow you to snug the base body close to the hook. Some anglers like to have that perfect top loop but building spinners on shafts with a closed loop will require a longer length of shaft above the blade.

Spinner Bodies

Spinner bodies provide the weight for the weighted spinner. They also provide the proper spacing between the blade and the hook. Even though the rotating blade is the main draw, the bodies can also provide a little additional attraction. There is a huge variety of spinner bodies and beads available to the lure builder. We won't cover them all and will mostly talk generically.

The length of the body components should be such that the bottom of the blade hangs down to the top of the hook. The weight of the body should match the blade size. If it is too light you won't be able to cast the spinner well or get down to the fish. If it's too heavy it will head to the bottom like an anchor and it will be difficult to keep it spinning.

Most bodies and beads are made out of brass. You can also build spinners using worm weights made out of lead, bismuth, and other metals. Plastic beads can be used for attraction and to provide additional length to the body without adding weight. Usually you start with the heaviest body and graduate down toward the blade. You always want a brass or plastic bead below the clevis. For in-line blades it's best to have a metal bead for the blade to spin against and solid metal beads will also be more durable for French blades. The bodies on in-line spinners will also be relatively shorter because, with the hole in the upper middle of the blade, they do not hang down as far.

Many styles of brass bodies have concave bases. These base bodies can be positioned very close to the hook. Smaller bodies are often tapered on the top and this helps you taper down to the clevis. The base bodies need to have a large enough hole to fit over the doubled wire. On smaller spinners with smaller base bodies the short piece of shaft will be bent over the top of the body and cut off. For larger spinners with longer base bodies you can just bury the short part of the open shaft into the body. Sometimes you will have to trim the short leg of the shaft to have it totally buried in the body.

Shiny bodies can be seen when the blade is spinning around and add to the attraction of the spinner. Most brass bodies are available in polished brass and nickel-plated finishes. You can also buy some that are plated with real silver. Usually I match the body finish with the blade finish. At one time, before they became available, I silver plated blades myself. I buy them already plated now because I can't consistently match the matte silver finish. But, I still silver plate brass bodies. You can get a reasonable silver finish without using an electrical current. I just dip them in a solution of sodium carbonate (1 oz.), silver nitrate (1/2 oz.), and sodium cyanide (1/2 oz.) dissolved in one pint of distilled water. Sodium cyanide is very poisonous and difficult to obtain. For most of you, the best plan will be to just buy nickel-plated bodies if the ones you want are not available in silver. They will definitely be close enough to real silver for the bodies.

Painted lead worm weights make good-looking spinner bodies and they can even save you money as they are much cheaper than brass these days. You can paint your own or have them painted. It is important to use a white base coat and lacquer, as a final coat, will make the finish more durable. While these bodies allow you to make a heavier body that is compact, don't get carried away and make your spinners so heavy that they don't spin well. You can also now buy painted brass bodies. With either metal you can jazz up your steelhead and salmon spinners with bright fluorescent bodies.

Hooks

While single hooks will work with spinners, trebles fit these lures better. It is easy for the blade of the spinner to create a path for the hook to be pulled out of the mouth of that prize steelhead or salmon. Round bend style treble hooks work well for spinners. Their wide gaps help you hook fish. Regular-strength trebles will work for trout and large fish much of the time. But after losing some large fish I have switched to extra-strong trebles. The cone-cut style by VMC has worked well for me. The mechanically-honed points seem to be more durable than the chemically-sharpened style. But if you have a favorite treble, by all means build your spinners with them. VMC has a vanadium alloy treble that is lighter than the normal carbon steel but just as strong. This allows one to use a slightly larger treble without putting the spinner out of balance. A good example is placing a number 4 vanadium treble on a size two spinner instead of the usual size six when fishing small waters for summer steelhead.

Whether you put colored tubing on your hooks or not is a matter of personal choice. I think that fluorescent tubing increases the attraction power of the spinner. For trout it might just get that following rainbow or brown to grab my spinner to get the "worm" that is trailing it. For salmon and steelhead the tubing just makes the spinner more noticeable. Tubing is available in vinyl or coated latex. Some of the latex tubing is quite rich in color but this tubing can become dirty and sticky with time in your spinner box. For that reason, opaque fluorescent-colored vinyl tubing is my first choice. I use straight red-orange on the trout spinners and a combination of two fluorescent colors on most steelhead and salmon spinners. Don't forget to put the tubing on your hook before making the spinner—it's definitely too late when you finish the top loop.

When regulations require single hooks, Siwash hooks can be used for large spinners for steelhead and salmon. While these hooks unbalance the spinner slightly they will still work fine. You will miss a few more fish that strike your spinner but they hold fish better than trebles once hooked so it balances out. You will want to shorten the bodies on these spinners because of the longer shank of the Siwash hooks. For smaller spinners I suggest using trebles with two of the hooks cut off. Start with trebles one or two sizes larger than you would use if employing the whole treble hook. Trim the hooks near the shank of the treble leaving a slight amount of the beginning of the bend. Then when you put tubing on the hook, it will not slide down

to the bend of the remaining hook. For Siwash hooks you need to use smaller-diameter, stiffer plastic tubing to keep it from sliding down into the bend.

You can also dress your hooks with fur, feathers, and synthetic materials. Another option is combining a fly with your weighted spinner. By doing this you create the illusion of something chasing the spinner. I have had considerable success combining streamers tied as tube flies with spinners. You can make the fly the body of the spinner by using metal beads and a cone head as part of the tube fly. The whole spin-fly can be made on the spinner shaft or you can complete the fly separately and place the spinner blade on a plastic clevis that will revolve around the leader. No matter which way you make them, you will always want to have a plastic or metal bead between the clevis and the tube fly. There is no limit to possibilities when combining spinners with flies.

Putting Them Together

Now we are going to put some model spinners together. These are all spinners I fish with on a regular basis, except for the size zero. Many anglers like the size zero and use them in small creeks for diminutive trout. When I encounter a clear small-stream situation I usually opt for a very tarnished brass or copper number one spinner instead of a zero because the ones are just a little easier to get spinning and that is important in tight quarters.

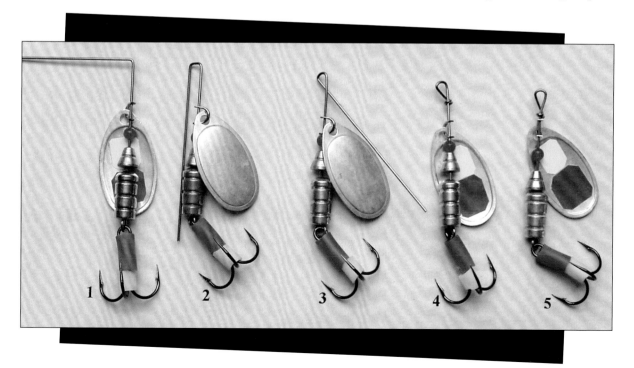

SIZE 0—Hang a size 10 treble (with red tubing) on an open-wire shaft. Slide a 7/32-inch solid-brass bead over both wires to close the loop. Bend the short wire over the bead a bit past 90 degrees and trim it close to the bead with diagonal cutters. Slide a 3/32-inch-diameter hollow metal bead on the shaft. This bead acts as a spacer and helps the next bead sit level rather than be tilted by the bent-over wire shaft. Next slide a 3/16-inch solid brass bead on the shaft. Now hang a zero blade on a number one or two clevis and slide onto the shaft with the concave side toward the shaft. With needlenose pliers make a right-angle bend in the shaft about 5/8 of an inch from the clevis (Step 1 in the photo page 57). Then move the pliers just the width of the tip of its jaws closer to the clevis and make another right-angle bend (2). Place this squared off end in the jaws of the pliers and squeeze. This will round the squared end and cause the wires to cross (3). Now is the time to build a swivel into your spinner if you desire. Put a size 12 or 14 black swivel for small spinners or a size 10 or 12 for large spinners onto the rounded end. Now wrap the wire one and a half times around the shaft and trim off the end with your diagonals (4). Align the loop so the rounded end is directly in line with the shaft (5). It's important to use needlenose pliers with parallel grooves rather than cross hatches so you can grip the wire. You can also use jeweler's pliers and wrap a loop around one of its round jaws. Wire-bending/spinner-making tools are also available but I find it easiest to make the top loop as described above.

SIZE 1—Hang a size-8 treble (with red tubing) on an open-wire shaft. Slide a 1/16 oz brass body over both wires and bend over the shorter wire and clip. Slide a 3/32 hollow bead followed by a 3/16 solid brass bead. Hang a number one blade on a number two clevis and slide on shaft and make the top loop as described above.

SIZE 2—Hang a size 6 treble with red tubing on an open-wire shaft. Slide a 1/16 oz. body on to close the loop and bend over and trim wire. Slide a 1/32 oz. conical body (commonly called a "T" body) on to the shaft. Then slide a 4mm red bead followed by a number 2 blade on a #2 clevis and complete the top loop.

SIZE 3—Hang a size 4 treble with red and chartreuse tubing on an open wire shaft. Slide a 1/8 oz. body on the shaft to close the loop after pre trimming the short wire on the loop so it's the same length as the body. Slide on a 1/32 oz. conical body and then a 4mm red or chartreuse plastic bead. Hang a number 3 blade on a size-2 clevis, slide on the shaft and complete the top loop.

SIZE 4—Hang a size-4 treble with two colors of tubing on an open-wire shaft. Slide a 1/8 oz body on a pre-trimmed shaft to close the loop. Add a 1/16 oz tapered brass body with the smaller end on top. Add a 5mm plastic bead and then a #4 blade on a size 2 clevis. Complete the top loop.

SIZE 5—Hang a size 2 treble with two colors of tubing on an open-wire shaft. Proceed the same as a #4 but use two 5mm beads of different colors.

SIZE 4 Pb—Hang a size 4 treble with two colors of tubing on an open-wire shaft. Slide an 8mm chartreuse plastic bead over both wires. Slide a fluorescent orange painted 3/16-ounce lead worm weight over both wires. Slide a 5mm chartreuse bead followed by a #4 blade on a size two clevis and complete the top loop.

SIZE 5 Pb—Hang a size 2 treble with two colors of tubing on an open wire shaft. Slide an 8mm red bead over both wires followed by a chartreuse painted 1/4-ounce lead worm weight over both wires. Slide two 5mm red beads followed by a #5 blade on a size-two clevis and complete the top loop.

SIZE 5 Pb INLINE—Hang a size-2 treble with two colors of tubing on an open-wire shaft. Slide a 6mm chartreuse bead followed by an orange painted 1/4 worm weight over both wires. Slide a 5/32 solid brass bead on the shaft followed by a number five in-line blade. Make the top loop. All nine of these spinners are shown in the photo below.

While I don't use them, size 6, 7, and 8 spinners can be built like the size 5s using increasingly larger bodies and more beads so the blade hangs down to the top of the hook. The above are all just examples of spinners I make and use. Please note that I never put a bead above the clevis. It is unnecessary and unless it's really tiny, water pressure against it will "pinch" the clevis, inhibiting the spin of the clevis and blade. One of the joys of building spinners is that you get to be as creative as you want. Then the fish get to decide if you have designed a winner.

There are a number of sources for spinner parts. We are going to list some of those with the most extensive offerings here. You may need to ask questions about blade thickness and body-hole diameters before you order. Also one manufacturer sizes its blades differently than the others. For example, their size 2 is about the same size the other's size 1. Many of the catalogs from the retail companies below have actual size charts but if not you may want to ask about the length of the blade versus size number. If you have trouble finding what you want or have questions about spinner building you can reach me at gairdneri@comcast.net or 517-484-5178.

Fisherman's Shack
9465 Airlie Road
Monmouth, OR 97361
www.fishermanshack.net

Jann's Netcraft
3350 Briarfield Blvd.
Maumee, OH 43537
www.jannsnetcraft.com

Pentac
Yroba, CA 96097
www.pen-tac.com

Stamina
8408 73rd Ave. N, Unit 40
Brooklyn Park, MN 55428
www.staminainc.com

R & B Lure Company
P.O. Box 1267
Fairview, OR 97024
www.randblures.com

Preventing Spinner Loss

Before we talk about hanging on to your creations it's important to acknowledge that by building your own at a fraction of the cost of the models hanging on the pegs at the tackle shop you automatically fish them better. You cast them closer to the fish holding cover because you are less worried about losing them because they didn't cost a lot and you will have an excuse to build some more flashing lures.

But it still doesn't make sense to donate too many to the snags. First, remember that spinners will draw strikes from a considerable distance so don't try to get ridiculously close to the cover. Make the first cast near the log and then get the second one a little closer. Also keep in mind that trout and salmon look forward and up so you just need to have your spinner near the bottom. When you feel the blade on your spinner tick the bottom, lift up a bit with your rod. Be observant and follow the casting tips presented earlier. The worst place to lose a spinner is in a tree or other streamside vegetation. There is no chance to catch a fish there, and you can't say you didn't see the "snag".

Inevitably you will hang-up your spinner, usually many times on each outing. If you snag-up on the bottom downstream from your position on a sweep cast you can often use the current to dislodge the lure. Simply release five or six feet of line into the current and then jerk hard. Due to the belly in the line you will be tugging on the lure in the opposite direction and free the spinner. Wherever you hang up your plan should be to get on the opposite side of the hang up before you pull hard to dislodge the spinner. We let the current do that when the spinner was below us but will have to change our position for upstream and quartering upstream presentations. If the initial jiggling and pulls don't free the spinner it will be time to pull hard and either bend the hook to free the spinner or break it off. It is very important that you point your rod at the snag and pull very slowly. You need to give the hook a chance to open up. This slow pull will almost always cause the line to break at the knot if you can't bend the hook. If, by accident, the line should break in the rod don't leave all that line in the river. Tie on another spinner and try to snag the trailing line and bring it to you. Then, try again pulling slowly to break the line at the knot. You might even get lucky and free the spinner on the second try.

If the water is wadeable to the spot where your spinner is hung up you can keep your arm dry by using your rod to dislodge the spinner. Pull back on the line with your free hand until the rod tip reaches the spinner. Then gently push the spinner off the snag. Don't pull on the spinner, that's the way it got hung-up in the first place. Always remember that you are trying to dislodge the lure by going in the opposite direction.

It doesn't make sense to eat into your fishing by taking a long time to free a snagged spinner. However, it also takes some time to tie on a new lure so try for a minute or two at least to free your lure.

CHAPTER 11

Landing & Releasing

Landing big fish is always a challenge when river fishing. And big is a relative term depending on your tackle and size of the stream. A wily two-pound brown can get you in trouble in a small brushy creek when hooked on ultralight tackle. Large steelhead and salmon can find a way to escape even when hooked on fairly heavy tackle in a relatively open river.

Releasing most of our trout and steelhead, especially wild fish, is important for the future of our sport. While Pacific salmon are at the end of their cycle when they make their spawning runs it's still very critical to allow enough fish to spawn the next generation. Proper tackle preparation is a key component to landing steelhead, trout, and salmon in the rivers and streams, and the way you fight and land your fish plays a big role in their successful release.

Hooking, Fighting and Landing

The fact that you can use fairly heavy line when spinner-fishing would seem to making landing big salmonids a piece of cake. Well, after 45 years of chasing trout and steelhead, I can testify there are plenty of ways for these fish to fail to get hooked and escape when they are hooked. Landing steelhead and salmon begins before you reach the river. Careful attention to your hooks, line, knots, and rod and reel is just as important as your fish-fighting tactics.

Since a highly castable line is important for successful spinner-fishing and, by nature, these lines are not as abrasion resistant as the tough, less manageable lines, it's important to check for frays and nicks and to change your line often. As described in Chapter 2, you don't need to refill the whole spool when changing your line. You can also extend the life of your working line by reversing it. After you have fished line for several trips and perhaps have slight abrasions or other damage, you can turn the line around so that you will have new line at the important end, near the fish. This process can also be helpful if a big trout or salmon rubs your line on a boulder or logs and slightly frays it ten yards up from your spinner. If you clipped off the ten yards then your casting would be impaired. Reversing the line is most easily accomplished while standing in the river. Just release line from your reel until you reach the blood knot. Make sure you have a good grip on the working line and cut the line at the blood knot. Now feed the good end and let it trail in the water as you work your way back to the frayed end and then retie the slightly damaged end to your backing with a new blood knot. An additional benefit is that you have relaxed the line and removed any twist. Of course, if the strength of the bad end of the working line has been significantly affected, you should just change spools.

Whether you tie on your spinner with an improved clinch, Palomar, Trilene, or, the new to me, San Diego jam knot, it's very important to test it before you cast. Lubricate your knot with saliva or water before you draw it tight and tighten it very slowly. Continue to check your knot as you fish. This is especially important if you have adopted my strategy of using a duo-lock snap so that you can change lures easily and without retying. It's also a good plan when fishing for large fish like steelhead and salmon to just automatically retie after each fish is landed.

Lynda Hayslette battles a rampaging steelhead.

Using premium-grade, extra-sharp hooks will pay off in more landed fish. Often these hooks are sharp out of the box but don't hesitate to put the stone or file to them if necessary. And check them as you fish to make sure the rocks have not dulled them. If a point is broken or the hook becomes badly bent and can't be reshaped it's best to change spinners and rebuild the spinner with the bad hook when you get back home.

Your rod and reel can also adversely affect your line if the guides are damaged or grooved or the roller on a spinning reel is not spinning or is also grooved. So this is something to check if you observe your line fraying or wearing out prematurely. Unless you are an oddball like me and back-reel instead of using the drag you will need to make sure your reel drag is operating smoothly and properly set. Keeping the drag set pretty close to the line test while fishing will help with the hook-set but it's a good idea to back off on the drag for the battle.

While trout, salmon, and steelhead may really clobber a spinner and take care of the hook-setting on the strike, it's important that you react with a strong lifting of the rod when they don't. After a good hard hook-set you can back off on the rod pressure if there is plenty of room to fight the fish. Unless your quarry is headed for a log jam or root wad you can relax a bit and enjoy the battle. Always try to stay as close as possible to the steelhead or big trout. Following it and keeping it on a short tether are real keys to landing big fish in streams.

The author weighing a steelhead in the net.

When there is considerable distance between you and the fish you lose control. For example, if a steelhead gets well downstream and decides to swim toward the bank where there are submerged logs you will have no leverage to prevent this from happening.

When a big fish heads toward the brush or logs early in the fight trying to stop it may not be a good option. Either the line will break or the hook will be pulled out when you put too much pressure on the steelhead or salmon. The better technique is to try and alter the course of the fish and steer it clear of the underwater obstacle or to your side of the boulder or bridge abutment.

If a large trout, steelhead, or salmon doesn't cooperate and makes it around the rock or log you need to immediately slack off on the rod pressure. Either give line by back reeling or open the bail on your spinning reel or put your casting reel into free spool. The friction of the line on the snag will keep the line tight to the fish while you try to work to free your line. If you continue to pull hard with your line around the obstacle, the salmon, steelhead, or big trout will break your line because there is no rod to cushion the line against the fighting fish. If you cannot wade or position your boat so that you can free the line then feed line so there is a belly of line below it might cause it to swim back out. Many times when this didn't work I have been able to wade below the log or brush and find my line with my wading staff. Then you can try to hand-line in the fish. If the steelhead or salmon is too big or has too much fight left for that option and is quietly resting you can cut the line, pull it free

from the log jam, and retie it. Of course it can be pretty nerve-racking tying the blood knot when at any time the big fish can take off and say adios.

The sight of a big steelhead, silver, or rainbow clearing the river surface is one we all enjoy. But this is also a time when we may part company, especially when using fairly hefty lures like weighted spinners. Drop your rod toward the fish when it jumps to take tension out of the line and then tighten back up upon re-entry. You can usually anticipate leaps by watching your line move up in the water column.

You can speed up the capture of the fish with lots of lateral pressure. A high rod position that is just lifting the fish will be mostly fighting gravity. Our advice on staying close also shortens the fight.

As your fish tires and it becomes time to land it, always try to get below the fish. I prefer to use a net because I think it's easier on the fish and speeds up the capture. It allows you to land a big trout or salmon in deep water and before it is exhausted. Positioning yourself below the fish allows the current to help push it into the net. Leaving your net bag in the water prevents injury to the fins, scales, and avoids protective slime removal. The net also provides a corral for easy unhooking. You can also resuscitate the fish in the net bag and then simply lower the net rim and allow the fish to swim free when it's ready.

At times you can also quickly land a salmon or steelhead by beaching it in shallow water. Again get below the fish and pull it broad side to the current so the flow can help push it into shallow water. Never try to beach a fish on dry land unless you plan to keep it. The bruising and abrasions that occur as it flops on the substrate are sure to injure the fish. While small fish can be quickly brought to hand, large trout, salmon, and steelhead will often exhaust themselves before they are quiet enough for you to pick them up. Plus, you will lose some fish trying to bring them to hand.

Releasing

Rapid capture, minimal handling, and gentle release are the obvious keys to the successful release of the salmon, steelhead, and trout that we love to catch. We've got the fish landed and now it's time to unhook the fish and let it go. All members of the trout and salmon family have sharp teeth so it's critical that you use hemostats, forceps, or needlenose pliers to aid in unhooking them.

The author releases a spoon-caught Babine steelhead.

Two bad things happen if you don't have one of these tools when the hook is well embedded in the fish's mouth. First, you are likely to nick and cut your fingers on the salmonid's teeth. Then as you struggle to unhook the trout or salmon with your fingers you are keeping the fish out of water longer than necessary, and may cause injury by squeezing the fish trying to hold onto it as well as removing more of its protective slime coat.

If the hook of your lure is near the edge of the jaw you can usually grab it with your pliers and twist it free without touching the fish. With spinners this will often be the case and you can just lower the net and let the salmon or steelhead swim off. There will be times however when the spinner is taken deeply and the unhooking is more difficult. While it is important to avoid the gills and eyes when handling these fish there are times when using the gill cover as a handle is the best way to unhook and release them. With a wet hand carefully slide you fingers along the gill plate and take a

firm grip. The back of your wet fingers may graze some gill filaments but will do no harm. Remember these organs are designed to slough off sand and silt and other foreign objects suspended in the water that pass by as the fish breathes. When using the gill cover as a handle the mouth will open up and let you see where the fish is hooked. Carefully push down to make room for the barb and then back out the hook. This will usually require pushing the hook deeper into the mouth. You can make this chore easier by flattening your barbs or using hooks that are barbless or have very small barbs.

There will be times when you hook a fish in the gills and break a gill artery during the fight or when unhooking the fish. This is often a fatal injury as fish have only a small amount of blood compared warm-blooded animals. So if it's legal to keep the fish then it should probably head for the table. If not then you should do the best you can to find a quiet spot for the fish to possibly recover. There is always hope and an especially decent chance if the water is very cold.

Several years ago I hooked a large lake-run brown trout in Michigan's Prairie Creek. It was gushing blood during the battle and I was sure it was a goner. While Prairie Creek was open for retaining steelhead, the season was closed for brown trout to protect the resident trout. So even though this fish was lake run it had to be released. Luckily it was December and the water temperature was in the low 30s. I found an almost stillwater spot and propped up the fish between two logs facing into the meager current and hoped for the best. In March, I caught this twelve-pound brown trout again in the next pool downstream from where it had been released. It had survived, hooray! Many anglers are of the mind that it's a total waste to release fish that might not survive. I disagree. Even if the fish dies it will provide food for other critters and provide nutrients to start the food chain again. And, if you keep the fish there is a 100% chance it will not live to spawn and possibly thrill another angler.

With small to medium-sized trout it's not necessary to use a net and often you can release the fish without touching them. Just kneel down and grab the hook shank with your forceps. The trout will usually twist free. If this maneuver doesn't work then cradle the trout in a wet hand and turn it upside down to keep it from struggling while you unhook it. It's important to note that a small amount of blood from the mouth of a trout or a larger salmon or steelhead, as opposed to the breaking of a gill artery, is definitely not life threatening.

If you want to photograph your catch it's important to get everything ready before taking the picture. Have the camera operator ready to hit the shutter button and then lift the big steelhead or trout out of the water and smile. Always cradle and support the fish with both hands. You are now also ready for a second shot of the release as you dip the fish's head back into the water.

Often it's fun to know the weight of your fish, especially if it's of exceptional size. An estimate can be done by measuring the length and girth but it's also easy to weigh the fish using your net. Simply hook your scale on meshes on opposite sides of the fish and weigh it as the steelhead or monster brown is cradled in your net. Then just subtract the weight of the net or suspend the net rim with your other hand while weighing the fish so that the rim is not being weighed. In recent years the style of hand-held scales with a gripper on one end has become very popular. I think weighing fish this way is very hard on them, especially large specimens. Fish are normally horizontal in water that is approximately the same density that they are. They use their swim bladder to maintain neutral buoyancy. While I know of no studies documenting the fact, I believe that suspending a large fish vertically in the air could harm the internal organs of the fish. This would be especially likely when the fish are on their spawning run and their sexual organs are near maturity. You can still use these grip scales to weigh fish supported in a net.

Always release steelhead and salmon into water with a gentle current when they show signs of being quite tired. Support them in the slow flow until they are ready to swim from your hands. Moving the fish back and forth is counter productive because the backward movement stops the flow of water through the gills. If there is no current then it's best to move the fish slowly in a forward direction through the water.

The obvious value of releasing fish is that they are allowed to spawn a future generation of their species. There is also a reasonable chance that they will thrill another angler. I routinely mark the trout I catch and release in some of the streams that I fish often. I do this by punching a small hole in their adipose fin. This fin is the small fin without rays just ahead of the tail on the dorsal side of all trout and salmon. It's the fin clipped by the mass-marking machines that mark all hatchery salmonids in the Pacific Northwest. In checking my log book for the last few seasons I found that an average of 16 trout were caught each season that had been marked fish. It really makes you feel good when a trout grabs your lure for a second time. This is especially true when the trout is caught again in the same hole and has grown significantly since it was released. Most of the time the mark will be quite healed, indicating that it took the trout a season or more before it was ready to go back for seconds on those shiny lures.

Trout, salmon, and steelhead make excellent table fare and you should never feel guilty about harvesting one of these fish where it is legal and the fish population is healthy. You will have the smallest impact on future generations by choosing a male for the table. A male trout or salmon can fertilize the eggs of several hens and often they try to do just that. Once you remove the female from the river you have lost that reproductive potential. Males also often make for better eating than the females when you are fishing for steelhead and salmon on their spawning run. Producing eggs takes more out of the fish than generating milt does and the flesh of the females will be paler and less firm even though it's more silver on the outside.

CHAPTER 12

Cast & Retrieve Alternatives

While I believe weighted spinners are the most versatile and effective lures for catching trout, salmon, and steelhead in rivers and streams there are times and locations where other lures that can be cast and retrieved are the better choice. In this chapter we will describe the where and why for choosing spoons and plugs instead of spinners.

Spoons

Spoons are a lot like spinners in that they are compact, easy to cast, and sink quickly. They also attract strikes from a considerable distance. We will focus on the highly bent, compact oval spoons like the Little Cleo and BC Steel as they seem to be the best for river fishing.

The oval spoons have less water resistance than spinners and thus require a faster retrieve rate to have action. Thus, they are not a good choice when fishing in relatively slow water or retrieving with the current. But this lower resistance and their heavy, compact nature make these spoons ideal for getting down in deep water and sweeping across heavy current. This is helpful in high-gradient rivers, especially for winter steelhead in the Pacific Northwest.

While I will switch to spoons at times to fish faster water they help me out the most when I am trying to make long casts to reach water I cannot wade close enough to reach with a spinner. My home river is Michigan's Grand, a large and wide river by Great Lakes' standards. I can cast the same-weight spoon about 20% farther than a weighted spinner. The reason is aerodynamics. The compact, thick spoon sails through the air with little resistance while the spinner blade tends to "flap" in the breeze.

You can build your own spoons just like you can spinners. It's really simple, just attach the hook with a split ring. Single hooks work best with spoons and the Siwash style works really well. These hooks hold fish very well and since they are automatically aligned perpendicular to the spoon by the split ring they also hook the salmon and steelhead very effectively. The point of the hook should always be positioned on the concave side of the spoon. Commercial spoons often come with treble hooks and have a split ring on the opposite end of the spoon. I think it's definitely a good idea to change the hook to a Siwash and take the other split ring off if you have adopted my duo-lock snap plan for quick lure changes.

Many commercial spoons have a stripe of paint while the blanks will be plain metal. I think adding some contrast makes the spoon more effective. I did take a lot of kidding though when I put a rectangle of fluorescent orange lure tape on the convex side of some silver spoons. Everybody wanted to know why I forgot to take the price tag off the spoon.

Plugs

High-action diving plugs like Hotshots, Hot-n-tots, Wigglewarts, and Kwikfish have long been popular lures for steelhead and salmon. Usually they are pulled against the current from a drift boat that is rowed against the current to slow it so that the lures dive and have action. These lures are also dropped back from an anchored boat. These diving lures can be cast and retrieved but they are limited to presentations against the current.

My spinner gets taken off the snap and replaced with one of these plugs in two key situations. The first is when a steelhead follows a spinner several times but just won't finish the deal. Putting on a plug and sweeping it by the fish is often just what it takes to get the interested fish to strike. If you can get above the spot where the steelhead or salmon is holding you can make the plug wiggle in place right in its territory. Be sure and hang on to your rod as the fish will often really clobber your plug.

Another situation where I will fish a diving plug is where a bush or some other streamside vegetation is draped over and laying on the surface of good holding water. I will get above and cast the plug just upstream from the brush on the surface. I pull the plug under the water and slowly back it downstream under the cover. You can sweep a spinner in front of these spots but it's hard to get it back underneath like you can a plug with the current's help.

Minnow-shaped plugs or stick baits have been fairly popular lures for stream-resident trout for a while but are just now being recognized as good steelhead and salmon lures. They still have more applications for trout and we will start there. One of the main reasons is that these lures perform well when retrieved with the current even though the best presentation continues to be across and down.

The incident that made stick baits a permanent part of my trout fishing arsenal occurred about five years ago and approximately coincided with my frequent use of the duo-lock snap. I was fishing a small southern Michigan creek and doing well catching good numbers of brown trout between 12 and 18 inches. It was with great anticipation when I arrived at the last hole in the reach because the trout were biting and this hole was the largest and deepest. I probed the hole with a dozen casts of the number one gold spinner that had been producing so well up to that point. Nothing happened, not even a follow. So I cut off the spinner and tied on a balsa plug. A giant trout tried to kill the plug on the first cast but I didn't hook it. The big brown hit the lure three more times before I finally hooked it. After a tense battle I had two feet of beautiful brown trout in my net.

Minnow plugs look more like real food to trout than spinners do and for that reason work real well in relatively slow water. I think the trout get a long look at the spinner in this kind of flow and while it looks alive they don't hit because it doesn't represent anything in their regular diet. Large trout of all species become fish eaters. They even eat their own.

Steelhead hooked with a minnow plug.

While trout usually try to grab and eat spinners they often try to kill or stun a minnow plug first and then come back to eat the injured "fish". So, while upstream casts and downstream retrieves with plugs will draw out the trout, hooking them is often problematic. When the trout comes back to grab the lure the current will have taken it away. Plus it's hard to resist setting the hook when the trout first attacks.

Whenever possible you should try to sneak upstream and get into position to make a quartering downstream cast when fishing minnow plugs. Retrieve the plugs slowly so they act like wounded or dying minnows struggling against the current. Occasionally pausing the retrieve is effective and adding an erratic twitching motion with your rod will often trigger strikes. If you fail to hook a trout drop the plug back downstream to the spot where the attack occurred and hold it there. Twitch it a bit without moving the plug upstream. If that doesn't bring the trout back, try moving it laterally toward the cover by extending your rod. I think it's best to use plugs that suspend but those that float at rest will also work.

In streams with good crayfish populations a plug that imitates them will often trigger takes when all other lures fail. When they are available, crayfish seem to be the favorite food of trout, especially good-sized brown trout. Your crayfish plug should dive well and make periodic contact with the bottom with its lip. Try to make it kick up some sand or debris from the substrate. Pausing the retrieve will also make the plug appear more life-like.

The addition of stick baits to my steelhead and salmon arsenal has been a recent development. Several years ago I witnessed an angler fishing with floating Rapalas at a popular fall fishing site on Michigan's Grand River. He hooked a number of steelhead while the rest of us were struggling to entice a strike. It seemed illogical that a lure swimming two feet under the surface would draw strikes from steelhead lying in five to six feet of water, but my eyes didn't lie.

While the stick baits will work anytime for anadromous fish, they seem to be especially effective when steelhead and salmon approach their spawning time. Fly-anglers have long been successful using the Egg Sucking Leech pattern when swinging streamers for steelhead and salmon. I was always of the mind that the contrasting colors of the head and the body were what made it more visible and attractive and thus so effective. This is likely still true but there may be something to the theory that these fish are indeed protecting or getting ready to prevent their eggs from being taken by small fish.

Plugs that are three to four inches in length work well for steelhead and salmon. Right now you will find Bomber Long A, Rapala Husky Jerk, and XCalibur Xt3 stick baits in my vest. These plugs dive to slightly different depths in the two- to four-foot range. They are also of different weights so I can vary my choice based on water depth and how far I have to cast them to reach the suspected holding water. As previously noted, even though most of these lures don't dive deeper than three feet they will still attract salmon and steelhead resting in six feet of water. This shows again that these fish look forward and up and will come up to strike a lure.

In addition to the shallow-running minnow plugs I also carry a couple of deep divers. These allow me to go deeper when necessary. I can still fish them in the shallower runs by slowing the retrieve and raising my rod tip. Fishing them in shallower water on purpose can pay off when the fish want more action at a slower retrieve.

Most plugs come with split rings attached to their tie-on eyes. You should remove these if you are using a duo-lock snap. Some deep-diving stick baits have their tie-on loops recessed into the lip and then I will leave the split ring to make it easier to attach the snap.

You can improve your success when fishing stick baits for steelhead, salmon, and trout by watching the lure or the area where you think it is located. As already noted these fish often make an initial pass at the lure without grabbing it. If you're keeping a close eye on the path of the plug you'll see a flash or possibly a surface disturbance when they do this. Try several more casts in the same spot to see if the fish will come back and nail the plug. If this doesn't happen, it's time to switch plugs or back to a spinner for another try. Obviously you have found an aggressive fish and you need to give it every opportunity to put a bend in your rod.

My favorite stick baits imitate minnows well and have dark backs and silver or gold sides. This makes them difficult to see on or in the water. Placing a small circle or oval of a bright orange or red lure tape on the top of the head of the plug makes it more visible. This makes it easier to watch your lure swim a couple feet under the surface and it also lets you see the lure as you float it down to a log or just the right distance above the lip of the tailout so you know when to start retrieving or sweeping your lure.

Adding some other cast-and-retrieve lures to your spinner arsenal can enrich your river fishing experience. Fishing will become more interesting when you study the water and try to decide which spinner or alternative lure would be just right. The duo-lock snap makes it real fast and easy to switch lures so there is virtually no time lost as you work your way up the river.

CHAPTER 13

Putting It All Together

The salmon, trout, and steelhead that we love to fool into striking our offerings are special fish. One of the charms of fishing for these critters is that we are never able to completely figure them out. They are biological organisms and as living things they will never be totally predictable. However, they are creatures of habit and we can adapt our angling techniques to their behavioral tendencies.

Dave Kaffke puts it all together on the upper Sandy with a spinner.

As we described in an earlier chapter, each trout or steelhead we catch can help us catch another one. As you work your way up the river on a given outing, always pay attention to where you caught a fish and then look for similar water and fish it with extra care. While it's usually easy to keep track of the types of holding water that produce on an outing it's much harder to remember how well a section of river produced last season or several years earlier. Keeping a fishing log or diary will help improve your success and enrich your angling experience.

Your diary can be as simple as writing down the stream and the catch on one of those calendars that has enough space for noting appointments, meetings, etc. with each day of the month. Or you can enter lots of details about the river conditions, weather, individual fish and where they were caught, even how many lures you lost, in a notebook or on special forms. It's important not to make the record keeping too much of a chore. It should be fun reliving the day while putting

down enough information to help you fish that section well the next time.

The pages in my fishing log book have spaces for just about all the information I can think of. But, I never fill in all the blanks. I will describe the parameters listed on my log forms and talk about why they are there and which blanks get filled in on a regular basis and which are usually left without entries.

My log book pages are designed for the listing of several outings and across the top there are spots for the date, weather including temperature and barometric pressure, stream and location, water conditions in & out, water temperature in & out, and the time when I started and finished the stretch. The main body of the page is for listing fish that are brought to hand or net. On each line you can note the date, species, its length, weight, & sex, the time caught, the successful lure, the rod, reel, & line, retrieve direction, cover type, bottom type, current speed, approximate depth, whether the fish was kept or not, and whether it had anything in

Lots of anglers think autumn is a great time to be on the river.

its stomach if kept. At the bottom of the form there is room to note my partners and their catch, approximate number of fish lost, number of lures lost, the driver, and an area for other information.

Let's go back over this laundry list and explain some of the categories. We'll also note the regularly

When it's your turn to watch the little one, you still find a way to go steelheading. (Doug Jones and son on Gnat Creek)

filled-in spots and the areas that seldom if ever receive entries. The top part on the stream and weather and water conditions is usually filled in fairly completely but with generalities. The weather might just be PC for partly cloudy. The temperature and barometric temperature and range of change will be noted. Water conditions will be mostly about height and clarity and any changes during the outing. If there is a U.S.G.S. staff gauge for the stream its reading will be entered. Water temperature will be noted at the beginning and at the end of the trip. The start and end time of my wade allows me to calculate the catch per hour and this can be compared to other streams and to previous outings on this stream.

When logging in the individual fish I always note the date, species and time caught but the other categories are less religiously entered. The lure is also always noted. For resident trout I will only enter fish greater than 10 inches and include the length but rarely the weight and sex of the fish. For steelhead the weight is a more important parameter than the length but it will often be estimated for fish under 10 pounds. The rod, reel, and line test are rarely ever entered unless I'm using something out of the ordinary. The retrieve is often just quickly noted by a D for down or A for across. The cover, bottom, current speed, and depth are not entered for every fish but patterns will be noted. If fishing for steelhead in a regular venue, the pool or run name will be placed in the cover column. Fin clips will definitely be written down when present and this is also the column where I note recaptures as evidenced by holes in the trout's adipose fin. Since I almost never keep a fish anymore the 'kept' and 'stomach content' columns remain without entries. Sometimes I will note crayfish when I can feel their lumpy presence when cradling a trout during unhooking. Also, I might note minnows, worms, or other food items that are regurgitated during the unhooking process.

Regularly summarizing the fish caught by your partners will provide more information about how the fishing was that day on that river. You might have a bad day when the fishing was okay and vice versa. I always take turns driving with my partners so noting the driver helps us remember who will have the next turn behind the wheel. This is especially helpful when fishing trips with some friends don't occur on a regular basis. Noting your fish encounters that didn't result in a landed fish gives you extra information just like noting how your partner(s) did. I categorize these fish encounters as follows (F), struck but failed to hook (FTH), and hooked but lost (L). Writing down the number of spinners lost may seem silly but it does give you an idea about how snaggy a particular reach might be when you prepare to fish it again. The miscellaneous information is for anything else that might have influenced your fishing or just made your day on the river different. You might note that there were lots of other anglers in your stretch of river. Or that there were a bunch of wood ducks that kept spooking ahead of you and landing in your favorite holes. A visit from an eagle, an otter, twin fawns, or some other wildlife encounter that enriched your day can be noted here.

One of the key elements to success with spinners for trout, salmon, and steelhead should be emphasized again as we near the end of this volume. Casting spinners allows you to accurately place your offering in the nooks and crannies of streams from a considerable distance. Take advantage of this and always fish with stealth. Do not let the fish know you are there. Keep a low profile and wear clothing that matches the background. Wade with long, slow strides rather than short splashy ones. Let the leap of a steelhead or roll of a monster brown with your spinner in their jaw be the first thing that disturbs the scene.

Finally, we are going to let a big brown trout make a couple more points that will further drive home tactics that will help you catch more fish. A couple of seasons ago I switched to a stick bait to fish a large open hole in a trout creek I fish often. The water was stained with a little over two feet of visibility so I put on a bigger minnow plug than usual for this small creek. On my second cast a large trout grabbed the lure and the battle was on. With lots of room to fight the fish I wore it down and got it into the net. It was a beautifully colored male that measured a full 24 inches. I carefully unhooked it and punched a hole in its adipose fin. About two months later I fished that same stretch of creek again. This time the water was low and clear. I probed the stream with a tarnished brass number one spinner and managed to catch several foot-long browns. I came to a bush whose branches covered half the width of the creek and retrieved the spinner as closely as I could to it. It seemed like part of the bush separated and attacked the lure. Twice the brown made it back under the bush but never did hang-up my line. By some miracle I corralled the fish in my net. It looked familiar; sure enough there was a hole in its adipose fin. The two-foot male had moved about 200 yards downstream from where I caught it the first time.

This fish exemplifies the resident trout's need/desire for cover. In spring the high, stained water made it possible for the lunker to hang out in an open hole with just enough water depth for cover. Once the water dropped and became crystal clear the fish sought a solid roof over its head under the bush even though the water was only a foot deep. With no leaves on the bush there was not enough cover to hide him in the spring. So always keep cover on the front burner of your angling mind. While it is usually more important to resident trout it's also sought out by anadromous fish.

Being prepared to switch lures to match the water types you encounter is also a key to success when river fishing for trout, salmon, and steelhead. Not only did switching lures to match the conditions help me catch the trophy brown twice but it's unusual to recapture a large brown during the same season on the same lure. So employ that duo-lock snap on the end of your line and be ready to adapt your offering to the holding water at hand.